simple &
the true subject of this book   *mind?*

STILL WATERS

prayer of the emerging quieter
self = gratitude Thanksgiving

p. 7
" My mind is such a hodgepodge
of spiritual data & 1/2 digested
ideas...."

p 14 "greatest heresy"
deepest wound" (sins of total
separation) (addiction to a
false self)

atonement - unity of feeling,
(at - one - ment) agreement, concord
w. others

Co. ditioning - I am "supposed"
to be comfortable but controllable;
were; that I have "needs";
that I am separate from
natural world, estranged

It is not what we go
thru that's important.
it's what we see thru..

See p 118 — vector
of causes → effects
p 120 just CONNECT

p.46

STILL WATERS

'One struggle at times is to
see that things, right now, could not be
any other way. When we can see that,
we can be
happy

Sobriety, Atonement, and
Unfolding Enlightenment

Internet

Christian doxology (?)
" that most Buddhist
of Xtian liturgy "

Kan's Koshers

WILLIAM ALEXANDER

Liv'g humbly we are unlikely to
compare + compete —
Comparison, competition (+ envy)
give rise to self-centered
fear, that creates a life
of persistent dissatisfaction
+ longing + sense of " I'm not
enough."

◼ HAZELDEN®

" nearly unbearable gulf.
between parent + child "

Hazelden
Center City, Minnesota 55012-0176

1-800-328-0094
1-651-213-4590 (Fax)
www.hazelden.org

Library of Congress Cataloging-in-Publication Data
Alexander, Bill, 1942–
    Still waters : sobriety, atonement, and unfolding enlightenment / William
Alexander.
        p. cm.
    ISBN-13: 978-1-59285-348-9
    ISBN-10: 1-59285-348-X
    1. Alexander, Bill, 1942– 2. Spiritual biography—United States. 3. Recovering
addicts—United States—Biography. I. Title.

BL73.A53A3 2006
616.86'10092—dc22
[B]   2005052818

This book shares the personal experiences of the author. In some cases, he has
changed names and circumstances to protect the privacy of his friends and family.

The epigraph is the author's version of the first lines of verse eight of the *Tao Te
Ching*.

T'ao Ch'ien, "Drinking Wine (Part 6)," translated by David Hinton, from *The
Selected Poems of T'ao Ch'ien.* Translation copyright © 1993 by David Hinton.
Reprinted with the permission of Copper Canyon Press, P.O. Box 271, Port
Townsend, WA 98368-0271.

Cover design by David Spohn
Interior design by Rachel Holscher
Typesetting by Stanton Publication Services, Inc.

This book is dedicated to my son, Will,
and my daughter, Kamala.

The highest good
        is like water
Water profits all things
        yet does not struggle

TAO TE CHING

Contents

Acknowledgments

My connection to the Empty Bowl Zen Group of Gainesville is a nourishing one. Thank you all.

I offer gratitude to my late parents, Bill and Nell, and to my brother, Phil, and all the ancestors.

I'm particularly grateful to the dedicated translators and poets who have worked to keep alive the words of the great lineage of Asian poets and teachers, with special gratitude to the efforts of Red Pine and David Hinton.

At Hazelden, Becky Post and Elene Loecher continue to provide inspiration and love. In Gainesville, Paul Linn offered an open mind and gentle voice to keep me on track and I am grateful for that.

Nadja Van Ghelue, thank you for your deep dedication to the ancient ways.

Finally, a deep bow to the ineffable teacher, endlessly realized in the most ordinary of things.

Introduction

I signed the contract to write this book on February 17, 2005, in the presence of my editor, Becky Post, and two of my closest friends, Lenny Holzer and Elene Loecher. We were in the dining room of the Renewal Center at the Hazelden treatment center in Center City, Minnesota. It was a brilliantly cold day. Ice crystals blew in the wind and the sun was glorious. As I signed the contract, at dusk, anything seemed possible.

A month later, I received the first part of my advance payment for the book and sat down to begin writing it in earnest. I cleaned my office. I bought a table for the computer so that while I was writing I could look out the window at the live oak and scrub pine trees that surround Hogtown Creek. I bought a new printer. I scavenged my bookshelves for reference material about alcoholism and recovery. I brought out books of poetry that have inspired me over the years. I even burned a CD to listen to as I wrote—mostly John Coltrane, Lucinda Williams, and Fred Neil, with a smattering of Gillian Welch, Elvis, and Louis Armstrong.

I spent a weekend at the beach with an old friend to be inspired by the seascape and the solitude.

I was ready to go.

But first I had to reorganize the kitchen, reposition the

hammock in the backyard for optimal wool-gathering time, and then move all the superfluous books out of my bedroom, leaving behind only the Bible, Red Pine's masterful translation of the *Tao Te Ching,* the *Bhagavad Gita,* and a book of cowboy poetry.

I was finally ready to write. I assembled my notes. I sat at the desk. The sun was dappling the deep green growth of spring, that juicy time of infinite possibility.

Three days later, I wanted to quit. I felt inadequate and incompetent to write such a book. This was some ten years after finishing a different book I wrote on the same subject.

I realized I now had far more questions than answers. The process of recovery from alcoholism was mysterious to me; a miracle I couldn't possibly understand. That, after all, is the nature of miracles.

How to approach the ineffable? How to point at a mere reflection when I had seen the moon? How could I possibly be serious and smart about what was, in fact, joyous and happy and free? What the hell did I know?

I wished I was a poet so I could just open the door and let you, the reader, in. But I write prose and often just stand in the doorway and describe what's on the other side.

I sat in meditation with this ugly situation. I realized that what I wanted more than anything else, at age sixty-two, was to remain Peter Pan, with a good boat and a tiny fairy to keep the sharks and the pirates at bay. This is truer than you can imagine. I was thinking hard about building a tree house in the Corcovado wilderness area of the Osa Peninsula of Costa Rica, buying a boat—a Boston Whaler—and spending long days fishing for my dinner (red snapper preferably) and nights, with the animal sounds of the jungle surrounding me, bringing to consciousness and paper the novel that still whirred in my head.

It's an old story, this busyness to avoid seeing the truth, and it is deeply embedded in my addictive mind. My conditioned strategy is to avoid difficulty and uncertainty. For many years, alcohol and other drugs were the tools I used in service of that strategy. When I finally put them aside, there was still the fear and still the strategy. I have used other substances—food and nicotine specifically—and I have used the insubstantial—intellectualization and bogus spirituality principally—to continue to stay firmly on the shadowy outer edges of the truth.

It was all I knew. There persisted, nonetheless, an inner knowing of both my fallible and my divine nature. The angels wouldn't leave me alone. Through spiritual practice I had seen how insubstantial this small self of mine was. I had been told that this self was in fact a delusion. I had experienced the reality of the true self, the unified one, on several occasions. At moments more vivid than any when I was regularly using hallucinogenic and psycholytic drugs, I had known that I was not separate from all the warp and woof of this beginningless and endless creation.

How had I moved from a life of reckless folly to one of inquiry and joy? When had I chosen love over power? What value was there in my endless failures and equally endless resolution to live a life of what the Chinese recluse poet T'ao Ch'ien called "simple-hearted contentment"?

The signed contract hunkered on my desk. The black notebooks I write in sat beside the stacks of books. I had plenty of pencils. I had a deadline and I had made a promise, to Becky and Elene and Lenny. Fellow writers stood by to read the upcoming drafts.

What to do?

Tell the truth, perhaps? Confess that this careworn creature that had spent decades of maudlin roaming in the boneyard of his own mind had become joyous?

During the early 1980s, when I furtively spent my days roaming the alkie bars in the Bowery in New York City, I learned the mantra and the curse of the dead-end alcoholic: *If something good happens, don't talk about it. It will go away. If something bad happens, it's your fate.*

It's time, twenty-five years after turning my back on the Bowery Curse, to let it go entirely. The only way I know to do so is to tell you the truth.

The truth is that I am happy. In the pages that follow, I will point to the path of simple-hearted contentment as directly as I can. I stepped onto that path in the middle of my twentieth year free from alcohol and other drugs. It was always there.

In the pages that follow, I will tell some stories and I will share some strategies for contentment. I will not tell stories that place blame or that are critical of those whose behavior has caused suffering. At times in the past, I have fallen into the ego-centric trap of blaming my family or my culture or my genetic makeup for my disease. There is some truth in all of that, and more, but now I see that I alone have the responsibility for my actions and the results of my actions. There will be a few brief family stories but the larger story of my family's life is my business, and to make this book a family biography would be to indulge in a kind of exhibitionism-by-proxy that I find unpleasant to read and to write. I will honor the love of my deceased parents by loving them back.

As to the larger culture and my genetic conditioning, I have no interest in that as "cause," only as contributors to my addiction; the why of it is not as important as what I did with it, this addictive beast within. I look at such tales as I may tell about that with a skeptic's eye, I reckon. I thought that this is a dangerous illusion; somewhere there is the cause of the plague of addiction and in the cause is the cure. Who cares?

What I could not have known as I began this little book is that in the course of it I would uncover those primal roots of my addiction, not in family history or science or a longing for God. These roots were revealed over many years of unbidden inquiry, and all at once, propelled by fear and faith in equal measure.

A Zen master once said that the secret of the Buddha Way is to pay attention. When asked again, he said, "Pay attention, pay attention." On the third repetition of the question, he shouted, "Pay attention, pay attention, pay attention." By coming unstuck from my expectations and desires, I was able to pay attention to the small details. It is not, in my experience, "all small stuff." It is in the small stuff, attentively and dispassionately encountered, that I find God.

Legend tells us that a vampire can never enter a home into which he is not invited, however eager he may be to tell his tales of exotic lands and to offer unique experiences. Once invited, and only once, he can then return willy-nilly, at any time, invited or not. The vampire paves the path through the front door and so charms his hosts that they welcome his visits. Once his intentions are clear and things get a little messy around the house, it is too late to rescind the invitation. I invited the vampire in on a Boy Scout camping trip in 1955 on an island off the southern coast of Florida. He came in a bottle of sherry. No night was ever so splendid, with stars close enough to touch and dear friends with whom to share the wonder of this new world.

I spent decades trying to repeat that one experience.

I had entered the world of the beasts and I would stay there for twenty-seven years. In the company of beasts, I quickly became a beast myself. This vampire—this morally neutral shaman—would take me to places I had never imagined could exist. The shaman owned me. The shaman made my decisions for me. The shaman was lover, confidant, and a wizard of oblivion. He was my rider on an ashen horse.

I wonder how my life would be, if only, if only, I could believe that this destroyer was anyone other than me. I cannot. He was created out of the dusts of antiquity, the bloodlines of my beginningless heritage, and the absolute reality of my life, right here, right now. This beast lives in the very cells of my body, as present today as he was fifty years ago.

I gained and lost the world twice during that time. I destroyed two marriages, lost contact with my beloved daughter, and razed three different careers. I was hospitalized numerous times and spent time in two psychiatric wards.

". . . bump, bump, bump, on the back of his head."

As a child, I loved the stories of Winnie the Pooh, but the often-quoted line above, from the very first volume, is not about Edward Bear being dragged down the stairs at this moment. It is, sadly, me being dragged out of a car again and into a hospital again, as a direct result of my alcoholism and drug addiction. Like Edward B. and his multiple trips down the stairs, I had come to believe that the only way to enter a hospital was by being dragged there. The time I refer to was in 1977, when I was thirty-five. I had drunk white wine on top of Antabuse. I had taken the Antabuse in a desperate attempt to get sober. It was the first of two times that I would drink on top of Antabuse and get dragged to the hospital. Those were only two of the many visits to hospitals that I made.

The truth is that by eighteen, I was already an out-of-control, crazy alcoholic, living for the booze that gave me meaning and sustenance. By nineteen, I had lived with material witnesses in a murder case in Houston, in a brothel in Juarez, and in a shack near Tampico, Mexico. I had killed tarantulas in a banana warehouse and was fired because I wasn't good at it. That day that I was fired I had enough money to get to the beach, where I put all the rest of the money in an ashtray and burned it. The next morning, I came to on the beach with a massive hangover from tequila and in amphetamine psychosis from the over-the-counter Benzedrine I had eaten like candy for six weeks.

By the end of my nineteenth year I had been in places where it wouldn't have been surprising to see a hog walk by with a snake in its mouth. The delusion, the greed, and the rage were well set before I was twenty. Twenty-two years of deepening madness lay ahead.

What is the point of telling this? In some places, it is not fashionable to tell these "low bottom" stories. They can be seen as romanticizing the addiction or of playing a "sicker than thou" game. Not so. If I don't tell the truth, I will forget the truth. If I forget where I came from, I can easily go back there. All it takes is the illusion of power and one shot of brown whiskey.

However, to dwell in those stories of depravity is not very useful. The constant repetition of a memorized story can become just an extension of the illness, a dogged attempt to find glory in corruption. In such a case storytelling turns to just another addiction, one unconscious moment at a time.

I won't tell such stories again, in full, in the course of the book ahead. There will be glimpses into my personal abyss, but I will not dwell there. I've made my point as well as I know how. I lived as a beast among beasts, the contents of my loving mind hidden at all but the briefest moments. I am done with that now. I need to take the risk of telling you about joy rather than decadence, a peril for any storyteller.

I hope that you will be a willing witness to joy and love and simple-hearted contentment. We will only peek through the windows of the places I've been. There is no need to linger.

My company now is the Chinese and Japanese hermit poets and the gentle people, and I'm a happy man. There has been joy on the path and blood on the ground, but it's been a good trip all the way.

CHAPTER ONE

Atonement

Everything changes.

This is the second book I have written about alcoholism. I wrote the first one nearly ten years ago while living with my wife and our children in the genuine beauty of the New Jersey that is not the butt of bad jokes or the setting for a TV series about crime families.

Things have changed considerably since I wrote that first book. I now live by myself in northern Florida. My parents are both dead, whereas during the writing of the previous book my mother was still alive. I bought their house from the estate. That's where I live, alone with a rescued cat that my son, Will, now a New England preppie, named Fred. Fred's a good partner. To the best of my knowledge he doesn't drink or use narcotics, although he does stay out all night at times. My dogs have all died, spending their final years on my former wife's dog-friendly property in New Jersey.

I'm slower than I was then. I can't touch the rim of the basketball hoop now and I can barely run at all since popping out my knee while training for a marathon. In that previous book I said that one of my dreams was to own a Ford F-150 someday. That's one of the dreams that came true. I bought a used one and then gave it to a friend a few years later, after a crushing divorce and just before my move to Florida.

Ten years ago I was a practicing Zen Buddhist. I still meditate daily but my practice has been deeply influenced by the old Ch'an masters of ancient China and their cranky, frumpy Taoist cohorts, such as Chuang Tzu and Lieh-Tzu, along with the poets T'ao Ch'ien, Li Po, and others. Those masters and the hermit poets of China and Japan have, dangerously, taken the place of contemporary Zen teachers in my internal hierarchy. Zydeco dancing is central to my spiritual life now, while then I would never have imagined that, at my age, I would be able to take on such an activity. As you will see in the pages ahead, my spiritual practice has become more catholic, small "c," emphasis on the second syllable.

I wrote that first book while looking over a meadow, working only during the morning. There were peach trees outside my window and as I wrote I watched them flower, bear fruit, and then go barren and sticklike over the seasons. At this moment, I am writing quite late at night. My desk is a folding table and is set in such a way as to give me a daytime view of a forest of live oaks garlanded with Spanish moss. There are scrub pines and low flowering bushes between my modest office and Hogtown Creek, which runs by just out of sight, down a small embankment.

As then, so now, I hear only crickets and frogs at night. As then, so now, I am content with my life. It has not always been so over the past ten years. I have learned the hard way that it is the unbidden, unexpected changes, the ones I never would have wished for, that have changed me in ways I could not have foreseen while sitting, writing, and watching the peach trees blossom in New Jersey. Just ahead lay tyrants in my mind that were only beginning to awaken then. I've learned that the changes I make are small potatoes beside those unbidden ones.

Back then I was enamored of science. Now I have left the religion of scientism far behind and find my greatest teachers in books of poetry. Wallace Stevens and T'ao Ch'ien are my companions here as I joyfully navigate the downward slope. Then, in my early fifties, I still dreamt the waking outlaw dreams of my childhood. Such dreams are transformed now and resurrected only from time to time as relics to ponder, from a life in a past that is still vivid but which is of only storytelling value to me now. I don't live in my past and those who do are welcome to it. There's more room since I moved out.

Then I was an active member of Alcoholics Anonymous and, to my chagrin, I wrote about that membership in ways that I now wish I had not. I still have a "desire to stop drinking," the sole requirement for membership in that miraculous fellowship, but I am no longer a member of anything that separates me from the larger community of my fellows. I am not "a" anything. I am not defined by my neuroses, my congenital conditions, my spiritual practice, my club memberships, or my social standing. I am an "earth person," a term used in the community of recovery, which creates a "them and us" division that I find deeply troublesome. I stake my claim on the earth, as you will see in the pages to come.

I have not had a drink since June of 1984. For that same period, I have not used amphetamines, Dilaudid, cocaine, Percodan, hallucinogens, Valium, or any of the vast pharmacopoeias that so ruinously occupied me for nearly thirty years.

I know less now than I knew then, but what little I know, I know well. My knowledge is tempered by experience and was cooked in the cauldron of my ordinary life.

If you read my previous book, you will find some familiar places in this one. Medon, Tennessee, and the Cathedral of St. John the Divine are two examples. But my awareness of those places and what happened there has changed considerably in ten years. What I once saw as pastoral and joyous, for example, I now see more closely as a place with ancient evils amidst the honeysuckle. The places haven't changed but my understanding has.

Here is my inspiration and the light to penetrate the dark places yet ahead. It is, typically, musical.

The four sections of John Coltrane's masterpiece "A Love Supreme" are (1) acknowledgement, (2) resolution, (3) pursuance, and (4) psalm. That describes my spiritual life better than I can. I lived for forty-two years before I acknowledged my multiple addictions. The resolution of these addictions took another couple of decades and continues, as pursuance. I think of pursuance more comfortably as constancy; the reality of being on the spiritual path, continually letting go, lightening up, and moving on.

This book, I think, is one long, very secular, and often irreverent psalm. I am bold in this claim as the book is not really a psalm at all, in the traditional sense. How could it be? It is not a song, certainly, and it is more profane than sacred, but it is a heartfelt expression of gratitude and uncertainty laced with bitterness and violence and peace and faith and devotion and, finally, at its core, with a startling and ongoing awakening to love.

I invite you to sing along.

The life of addiction is one of perpetual longing. That longing can continue for many years—for a lifetime—after the booze and the drugs are gone. "I want, I want, I want" is the chant of the discontented self. This longing is reckless and insistent. It will never be fulfilled. There is not one thing, one feeling, or one idea that will satisfy it. "I want" is always followed by "more." It gets worse.

When the wanting is subjected to the will, it only becomes more insistent. The absolute and final and irrevocable vow to give up sugar is followed, within moments, by the aching need for Ben and Jerry themselves to walk into the kitchen and get right to work. When I say that I am through with romantic relationships, again, every comely woman I see falls under the scrutiny of my mate-seeking eye. That longing, in particular, is like a dog lost on the freeway, looking, looking, and looking for some way to get the hell out of the situation it's in and into something that will be safe. And warm. And satisfying. Forever.

My desire for stuff is relentless. When I moved to New York City from San Francisco in 1982, I carried everything I owned in a backpack and a borrowed suitcase. At this writing, in 2005, I live alone in a three-bedroom house and have way too many things. When I do throw some of this stuff away, or grandly donate it to a charitable institution, I then go get more stuff, just like what I just threw away. I have four omelet pans and three copies of the poems of Rumi. I will occasionally find a DVD that I bought and forgot about and never watched. I once bought a Harley Davidson motorcycle and turned around and sold it the same day. My mind is such a hodgepodge of spiritual data and half-digested ideas that I could have a spiritual sidewalk sale.

Here is the truth. No person, place, thing, idea, or relationship will ever bring lasting satisfaction and contentment. They will always fail. Yet the desire for contentment is ever present. What will scratch that itch? I got the first glimpse of the answer to that question quite a few years ago. Now, sober for twenty-one years at this writing, I am beginning to see the answer more clearly. Unlike the longing for succor outside of myself, this answer has grown in me, a jungle flower, beneath consciousness for seventeen years. I suspect it will take a while longer to bloom and longer yet for me to be able to let it go and dance, at last, in the vast ballroom of simple-hearted contentment (the true subject of this book).

In the fall of 1988, I had been free of alcohol and other drugs for over four years. What had at first seemed an epic battle against the foulest of demons—my gross addictions—was now a fact of a simpler life. Yet, I was discontent. On the outside, all was well. I was married, I was finding work as an actor, and financial problems that had plagued me for many years were a thing of the past. I had been reunited with my daughter after more than sixteen years of not knowing her whereabouts. I had joined a church. I was lifting weights regularly and was in the best shape of my life. Weighing a trim 175 pounds on my birthday that year, I bench-pressed 350. Cigarettes were a thing of the past and I ate well. It was autumn in New York, a time of subtle changes and great simple beauties in that rarely beautiful city.

However, something was missing. An aching emptiness in my gut wouldn't let loose. With my grosser addictions gone and my superficial fears abated, I was in trouble. After years of simple escapes and grinning masks fashioned from fancy and fear, I was as close as I wanted to get to some primal truth I had never asked to see in the first place.

What was missing?

I made an appointment to talk with a good friend, a man who had guided me through the first few years of my recovery and who had moved on to become a trusted friend and confidant; a priest who had confirmed me in the Episcopal Church. This was James Park Morton, who was then the dean of the Cathedral of St. John the Divine on the Upper West Side of Manhattan. I told him something was wrong, that I needed to examine it with him in order to see it more clearly. I had no idea what I was getting myself into. Unconsciously, I had turned over a rock in my soul that would never be turned back over again. I had unknowingly asked the primal question: "What's the meaning of it all?" Truth, still spectral and unaccustomed to the light, a thing more fetuslike than fully formed, was released from its dark place.

The night before I was to meet with the dean, I spent an hour or so with some recovering friends. I was asked, that night, to tell the story of my years of addiction and my brief time in the community of recovery. This gathering, like the one to follow the next morning, was in an Episcopal church, this one on the Upper East Side, on Fifth Avenue.

Here, at last, at this point in the narrative, I have the opportunity to say something I have always wanted to say.

It was a dark and stormy night.

I had taken a cab from my home on East Sixty-seventh Street, up Madison Avenue to Ninety-first Street. There was distant thunder and the rain attacked concrete and asphalt with a nonchalant zeal. Taxis rushed by, all bright-yellow busyness, and the occasional pedestrians ducked under awnings or trotted home to warmth and dry clothes. I pulled my coat up over my head and skedaddled down the rain-slick sidewalk to the church.

That church is a welcoming old building, so very churchlike. Such a building really wouldn't do as anything else, you know. Its proper name is the Church of the Heavenly Rest, but it is often called, by the unwashed such as me, the Church of the Overly Dressed. It was and it remains a place of shelter and potential. I had found what I needed, four years before, when I dragged my hurting body in there for the first time, alone and afraid.

There were perhaps fifty of us there that rainy night.

After chitchat and introductions, it was my turn to talk. At that point in my life, I was still too insecure to speak spontaneously without a script or a collection of phrases and ideas that I had used before. So, lacking spontaneity, I had become skilled at appearing to be spontaneous. Public speaking is not one of my problems. There are those, I know, who think that I should take a closer look at my public shutting-up issues. But back then I loved to talk and I was stuck in the same old story and would stay stuck there for several years yet to come.

I talked for perhaps twenty minutes, telling tales of reckless drunkenness and fright. I still felt a need to say, occasionally, at the end of some episode or another, ". . . and that meant, of course . . . ," so stuck was I on meaning.

As I talked nothing was different. It was still the same story, with the same practiced nonchalance and drama. The story hadn't changed, the church hadn't changed, the night remained stormy outside, and I was in a circle of familiar faces.

In an instant, a change took hold of me.

I suffer from "gephyrophobia." The word is Greek, simply enough, from the words for bridge *(gephyra)* and fear *(phobia)*. It hit me for the first time in 1979 while approaching the Golden Gate Bridge from Marin County, headed for San Francisco. When I saw the bridge looming in the short distance, I was seized by a numbing panic. I felt immobile from the waist down, I hyperventilated, and I was afflicted with a sort of tunnel vision, which distorted size and shape and space in the middle distance. My heart was thudding. I was afraid I might lose control of the car and plunge over the side of the bridge to the waters below. My friend Toni, who was with me, said that my fear was so palpable that she felt it as well. I made it across the bridge and turned the driving over to Toni, who drove me straight to my physician's office. My doctor gave me a refillable prescription for Xanax. Oh, good. Drugs! This fear is crazy, of course. But it was very real. For twenty-five years I panicked at the sight of a bridge. Then the attacks stopped. Today, that fear has blown away—dust on the wind.

Standing in the circle and talking to my friends, I had a moment of anxiety that mimicked my gephyrophobia. I had the tunnel vision, the paralysis, and the moment of hyperventilation. My friends seemed miles away and there was a light haze in front of my eyes. I caught my breath in a mini-hyperventilation. The episode ended as quickly and as abruptly as it had begun. To this moment I have never told anyone about it, especially my physician friends, as I have had no desire to have this moment reduced to mere brain pan disturbance. (More about that prejudice lies ahead.) I don't know if that moment was related to the one that followed, but I choose to believe that it was. You take your spiritual arousals as they come and follow them where they lead, it seems to me. I did find out years later that such spiritual moments are never the end of a process but always the beginning of one. I forgot that, in 2004, and it nearly cost me everything.

On this particular night, the brainstorm was followed by a sensation that I then didn't have the words to describe. As I looked at my friends, I saw a warmth and acceptance in their eyes that hadn't been there, it seemed, just a moment before. There was a knowledge that I was not talking *to* them, but *with* them. I felt connected; at one with them. It was not a familiar feeling. It was as if an infinitely gelatinous curtain between me and them had distorted my vision, indeed all of my senses. I am not a fan of what I think of as "fluffy bunny moments," with sweetness and light abounding. I find them to be dangerous and delusional. I am not a sentimental man and I am deeply grateful for that small bit of sanity. This night I knew, however, that something was different and that I liked it. There was no way to express it then; I merely felt it and it felt strange indeed.

The next morning I walked the three miles to the Cathedral of St. John the Divine on Amsterdam Avenue. The cathedral and its grounds are imposing and remarkably peaceful in the midst of the cacophony and rush of the Upper West Side. It is a campus of thirteen acres with a multitude of buildings and quiet places; quiet, that is, when the resident peacocks and peahens are not adding to the traffic noise on Amsterdam Avenue. It is the world's largest Gothic cathedral and has, for many years, provided solace in an atmosphere dedicated to social justice and the divinity of this great earth.

Jim Morton's office overlooked the grounds and was, on that day and every day I visited it, a visual feast of the divine and the ordinary. I don't think that anyone but Jim could have made it what it was. I don't think I want to see it now. There were friezes of saints, statues of *bodhisattvas* (the Buddhist holy ones), and a multitude of toys. In particular, there were dozens of articulated snakes of all sizes. There was a small stone sculpture of a dolphin, all curves and movement. There were stones and crystals, some of astonishing size and some just right to roll around in your hand while you sat in that holy space. There were stacks of papers and magazines threatening to cascade to the floor. There were books everywhere—shelved, desked, and stacked. Books about architecture here and the principal spiritual texts over there with poetry and history and reference volumes scattered in between. There were notebooks and legal pads and pens and pencils galore. It was a delicious mess, which, in my self-centered way, I assumed to be a clear sign of spiritual genius.

Jim was on the phone, with his back to me, when I entered the office. He was talking to a fellow cleric and I overheard him say that he was despondent about the continual erosion of membership in the Christian churches. He wondered if maybe they were becoming irrelevant. He finished the call and turned and saw me and greeted me with such exuberance and presence that I felt as if I were the only other person in the world. I have had the great fortune to spend some time, often only moments, with a number of great spiritual teachers. Uniformly I have gotten the sense of extraordinary focus and attention to just that moment. Eyes are not roaming the room while the mouth repeats pleasantries.

Jim and I moved to another of his desks (there were three) and sat, he behind the desk, me, the supplicant, in front. He started to speak, paused, and then got up, grabbed another chair, and came and sat right in front of me. Jim is a big man with unkempt hair and gentle eyes that see deeply. He was wearing his clerical collar and a brilliant blue shirt, the color of the Aegean in still water. He inquired about "the Queen" (my wife) and about all the "cookie gobblers" (her children). We chatted for a moment about such things and about why the hell I hadn't started working in the soup kitchen, backed up with a reminder to get my ass to church on Thursday mornings for matins. I think that perhaps my own rough nature gave Jim permission to unleash his infrequent profanities. Then we got to the matter at hand. My plan was to talk with Jim, at some length, about those aspects of my character that stood between me and my desire for contentment. I had mailed him some information about the structure of such talks, which are considered to take place with God, self, and another human being. I was there, I reckon, to admit my sins. That was the way that Jim had said he saw it and I wasn't going to question him yet.

He asked if I was ready to start and wondered what I wanted to talk with him about.

I was flummoxed. The singular event of the night before, that descent into a sensory whirlpool and the sudden and unfamiliar sense of belonging, occupied my mind so completely that I had nothing else to say. For the weeks prior to this meeting, I had assiduously written out my concerns: my behaviors and my fears, my guilt, and what I considered to be my gifts.

I was mute. Jim sat patiently, waiting and giving me the opening to say what was really on my mind. Imagine what might have happened had he grown impatient or, irresolute, had jumped in to take control of the situation. He simply sat there, opening a space that I could feel free to jump into. Time stretched and contracted in that warm room, dappled with sunlight and shadow. I noticed the snakes, vivid in their stillness. In the darkness, something moved.

I told him, in the best way that I knew how, what had happened the night before. There was the vertigo of being torn loose from that which kept me safe, and then rising, not falling, into an altered reality. There was the astonishing sense of not being separate from the others in that room.

Jim cracked a smile that split the air in that wonderful room. He said, "That was it." He told me that my "sin" had been the illusion of separation.

Sin?

I was a sinner?

No, no, no. I had had my fill of that kind of thinking, the eternal damnation of that creature, foul in the sight of God, who would go off to some rickety, hot place, all covered in boils and open wounds, and be whupped to the point of a second death by smirking demons. No thanks, not for me.

I got so stuck on the word *sin* that I didn't hear, in the beginning, the part about the illusion of separation.

Jim told me that *sin* simply meant *without* and more deeply, *without connection.* Etymologically, I think he had it wrong, but who cares? It worked for me. Going back to the Old English roots of the word, it implies offense or wrongdoing or misdeed. The church, in its affection for dualism, saw *sin* as a good foil for *holy.* As the years have rolled on, I have thought of the word *sin* as indicating "delusion" or, my favorite, "folly of the mind." I am far more comfortable with that, but on that auspicious day, in that sun-streaked office, with that holy man, "sin" was just fine with me. If he said so. It pointed at my greatest lunacy and my deepest wound.

I thought there was some "I" that stood separate and apart from the entire phenomenal universe. I was addicted to that false self. I sought to protect it and to defend its multiplicity of wants. If "I" got what "I" wanted then "I" would be okay. That is addiction, the craziness of thinking that there was something outside of me that, when I got just the right amount of it, would make me okay. That something was, of course, protean, mutating from martinis to motorcycles to marriage to money (and to flights of overwriting), an infant run amok on a demon's playground.

I thought I was separate.

I can recall riding in a huge dark car with my parents on a winter night in Princeton, New Jersey. It was, maybe, 1944. I was nestled up against my mother's fur coat. The streetlights strobed slowly. The tires hissed against snow. I remember knowing, wordlessly, that I was not *that,* my mother with her gray-smelling, comforting coat; nor *that,* my father carefully driving in the snow. I was something *else,* with boundaries of flesh and thought. So it began, the necessary sense of not other, but *me.*

My sin, my folly, my entirely human and fallible sense was that such separation was total. No connection. No connection when in fact, as I was to learn, sensually, many years later, I am inextricably joined with the entire dance, including the sketchy drapes of moss on the trees outside of my window, and the Magellanic Clouds, only dimly seen. The Buddha and St. John breathe together in this glassed-in office overlooking Hogtown Creek.

Jim went on then to talk about religion. We jumped around in the etymological fields for a while and we played with the idea of delusion, two children in a dictionary, figuring it all out. Finally we got real about it. Jim has a string of letters after his name that point to an enviable education. He started out as an architecture student, met a worker priest, and became one. But those letters are impressive. They aren't who he is. He is a man who is deeply immersed in the stew of this world, feeling his way, rather than thinking it. In his presence that day, I felt the reality of connection.

On that day, the scales were still thick on my eyes, but it was a beginning. I understood that I was not separate from you. Now I needed to truly own that. I had to move beyond knowing, to sensing and living the reality I sensed. That was the task. The how-to was yet to come. But there was hope. Denial is always preferable to despair. Despair is permeable to hope. Hope will break denial. Rock, scissors, paper. Every day now, I practice. I light incense every morning and pray to be useful. The next morning, every morning, more incense and more prayers and vows.

It ain't easy.

AA cofounder Bill Wilson said, "Is sobriety all that we are to expect of a spiritual awakening? No, sobriety is only a bare beginning; it is only the first gift of the first awakening."

The first gift of the *first* awakening! The first awakening is the acknowledgment of being an alcoholic, in Wilson's context. The first! The implications are joyous, aren't they? Ahead, after the long process of simply getting the booze out of our minds, are multiple awakenings or, to my thinking, a rolling awakening, or unfolding enlightenment. It begins with the simple acknowledgement of being an alcoholic. To acknowledge this is to own it, to see its truth, and not to see oneself as separate from that truth. It's the wedge in the door. The door is a heavy one. It will slam shut in a cocaine minute, without vigilance.

I didn't know, couldn't have known on that day, that the awakenings yet to come would all rest on the simple reality of connection and would all be exactly that connection, deepening until even the idea of connection could be abandoned entirely.

I asked Jim what the process was, how to do the task. I wondered how to rid myself of the years of folly and delusion.

"Atonement," he said.

Dammit!

First I have to see that I'm a sinner and now, of all things, I have to "atone"? Visions of Elmer Gantry danced in my head.

No, not Elmer Gantry but Burt Lancaster as Elmer G. I did not want that particular message of atonement, thank you, although the nights of booze in brothels looked pretty good, the way Burt did it, sweaty and grinning and as charismatic as the best of new age charlatans yet to come.

Jim talked for a while about the acknowledgment of our foolishness and our greater recklessness and depravity. He said that such defilements need to be examined, without judgment, and acknowledged fully. Acknowledgment again. The owning of our sins. To atone is to be at one.

The crushing of the delusion of separation is this at-one-ment.

The preferred definition of *atonement* in the *Oxford English Dictionary* is just that: "*at-onement,* from a now archaic word *onement* with the prefix *at.* It is the *condition of being at one with others. Unity of feeling, concord, agreement.*"

I had gone to the Cathedral of St. John the Divine that day with a certain purpose in mind. I wanted to get beyond the feelings of discomfort and uncertainty and to find a sense of contentment. What I found instead was that the spiritual life was often uncomfortable, uncertain, and, at times, painful. As T. S. Eliot says, to reach that state of complete simplicity, the price is "not less than everything."

The dark one and the cleric still dwelt in me; they do to this day and always will.

The end of isolation is a process, not an event, and it unfolds, day by day, I have seen, with often terrifying and, more often, mundane results. But love awaits.

I told a friend not long ago that I had finally given up on romantic love. My rootless life seemed to make it untrustworthy. He asked, "You're saying that romantic love can't be trusted?" I said I thought not and he assured me that I was right: romantic love cannot be trusted and, knowing that, we can fall, at last, into love.

CHAPTER TWO

Life Out of Balance

Life is a maze of turning points. As adults we often miss them, and in childhood they are rarely seen. We are at the mercy of others for many years, just as those others spent their earliest years playing an unrecognized game of follow the leader. My grandparents had parents who had parents, on backward to the original ancestors. There is an inconceivable web of external circumstances and internal learning, beneath consciousness, a bloodline of destiny, which binds us to the unknown and unknowable ones. In my beginnings are endless beginnings that preceded me. These ancestors of mine sat under the same heavens as I do, seeing gods and story. Like me, they moved through the seasons. They saw wars and times of peace. Every event in their lives informed mine. I am connected by blood, time, and space to them all and, by extension, to all those they knew and to all the small events of their lives.

How can I trace that bloodline? It did not begin in rural Mississippi where my mother was born, the grandchild of slave owners, but that place and that horror are with me. My father's small-town Tennessee life, as the son of a doctor and a poet, is not where it began. But I have that in me. There is only the thinnest tapestry of childhood memory available to me at a conscious level. I cannot possibly conceive of or understand all the myriad influences that made me what I am. I can only see the effect of those numberless causes. There is no blame in me any longer. I cannot, given my understanding of cause and effect—a neutral reality—stick accountability anywhere but squarely in my own life.

The great teacher Shunryu Suzuki was once asked the essential clever question of Western philosophy: "If a tree falls in the forest and there is no one there to hear it, does it make a sound?" His response was, "Who cares?" I told my son, Will, that story and he got it, at once. "In other words, who's asking the question, right?" Right!

The essential task in the process of inquiry is to search for the one who is inquiring. This process leads into and, finally, out of the very isolation of the separate self. Who is this who cares about the sound of a tree in a forest? We will look more carefully at this process in the next chapter.

Memory is uncertain at best, but I believe that the material that it presents is important, no matter how flimsy or how easily questioned. A friend once referred to the retrieval of any memory at all as "Rashomoning about," a clever reference to the great film, *Rashomon,* by Akira Kurosawa, in which a crime is presented from the points of view of all the central characters and, for good measure, a shaman. How different the same story is, depending upon the teller! The criminal is right, of course. As is the living victim and as is her husband, the dead one.

So please permit me to Rashomon about, wandering in my past as I have done so often in my linear, physical life.

I am, by nature and conditioning, a wanderer, as were my parents and theirs. That's the story I tell myself, but there is no need to get stuck in it. Nature, conditioning, and longings are all capricious and insubstantial. I have lived on both coasts of the United States and in many places in between. The nomads sing their songs of the itinerant life to me still. When I moved to Florida in 2002, I told myself it would be my last move. As of this writing, three years later and nearly sixty-three years old, I am moving to Costa Rica for a year or so, at least. Perhaps it will end there, this roaming life.

I was born in Knoxville, Tennessee, in 1942 and would be an only child until my twelfth year. We moved from Knoxville to Princeton, New Jersey, before I was one and then to Berea, Ohio; Battle Creek, Michigan; Winnetka, Illinois; and on to Coral Gables, Florida, by the time I was eight. At fourteen, hormones ascendant, I was carted off to Nashville, Tennessee, a funky, horny place with all manner of wickedness just below its genteel exterior.

In between moves there were long stretches of time on my mother's family farm in Medon, Tennessee. We went there for Dad to dry out and begin again his career in secondary education. I didn't know that part until I was an adult and saw Dad drunk for the first and last time. I never knew he was a drunk, only that he could be several different people in the course of a day. Those dry-out trips didn't take. Dad did not stop drinking until after I did, in 1984. His sobriety, without the aid of any program or discipline beyond his strong faith in God, was dazzling. There remained, nonetheless, the early conditioning of the absent father and the roving family.

One of the gifts of a life that includes meditation is that the membrane between conscious and unconscious becomes very permeable. Small sensory events have been causing long-buried memories to erupt, unbidden, since I began writing this book. I drift back to the past and then find myself wondering if those events are repeating themselves endlessly in my life today, chained by conditioning I don't understand. I find myself worrying that I am still repeating my father's "failures" with my son as I did, in fact, with my daughter during my years of drug addiction. I am grateful for those opportunities, when the memories erupt. At those moments and those moments only, I can see the past and heal it. I can see that I must change the future by changing my behavior in the present moment. The cyclical process of awakening brings greater clarity to those turning points in the past. What might have been hidden to me a few short years ago becomes more vivid as time and nonjudgmental awareness increase. That membrane is more easily penetrated.

Certain types of light will trigger memories of incidents from times past. Most prominently, the flat, weak white of moonlit winter nights. A few years back, I was in Vermont for Christmas. My girlfriend and I had driven up to visit her alma mater. It was bitter cold and on our first night there I couldn't sleep. We were staying with her former major professor, a Russian woman of deep Slavic temperament. During my insomnia I reckoned she'd have tea. She did, and I made myself a cup and sat by the kitchen window. The chilled winter light took me back to a time when I was six years old and living in Battle Creek, Michigan. My father was assistant superintendent of schools and my mother worked as a librarian. I was alone for most of each day, responsible for walking to and from school and taking care of my dog, Duchess, a fawn boxer whose life comforted me and whose death was a bitter time. I occupied myself as best I could during that period in Michigan. I often moved furniture around, creating what I thought of as "machines," which I then explained to a phantom crowd of visitors.

On that decidedly unromantic moonlit night in Vermont, in this particular unbidden recollection, I was, all at once, sitting on the staircase landing outside of my parents' bedroom. There was something very wrong with my dad and I was frightened. He had been away for a few days and when he came home he smelled funny, like corn, to my untrained senses. I had smelt that smell many times, when he came to put me to bed. But that night, something terrible had happened and I didn't know what it was. The sickly weak light barely lit the stairs. I heard murmuring behind the door and strained to hear it. I could not distinguish words. It was sandpaper on the heart, a sound of pain and fear. I wondered what I had done.

All at once, my mother opened the door and saw me crouching there. She raised her hand to me palm out, holding it in midair. "Your father is sick," she said. "Go to bed." I moved to leave and she closed the door. I stayed. Sick? I had heard of something called the flu and wondered if he was dying of it. What could I do to make it better?

The next morning, Dad came to breakfast and I welcomed

him like the hero he was to a small boy, with those hard biceps and that charming smile. I already knew not to ask questions. Nothing was said about his "sickness" of the night before.

This is the most vivid memory of what I finally learned, in 1969, was Dad's habitual episodic binge drinking.

Over the years that followed that icy night, when my mother would have to leave whatever town we lived in, in a great hurry, because Dad was "in a clinic" in some distant city where he had gone for his work, I never asked what had happened and they never told. By the time my brother was born, in 1954, I had learned how to read all the cues in what was unsaid and un-acknowledged. If Dad was sick, I was not to ask what had made him that way. When there were endless silences between them, following nights of sad arguments, I knew to be the one who was quiet.

I hid in books, feeding the family denial of disease and violence by my complicit silence. There existed in that family a conspiracy of ignorance. Such was my conditioning.

I read all the books that children read: the Hardy Boys, the Black Stallion series, all of the Oz books, and many more. I knew that if I kept my head down and stayed engrossed in anything other than the great and running sore on my family's body, I would be "a good boy."

I remembered as well, in that warm kitchen in Vermont, an event that occurred in 1967, many years after the staircase incident. I had returned to Tampa, Florida, from the Haight-Ashbury section of San Francisco and my first wife and I were trying to make a go of it. There had been real ugliness between us. She had divorced me, but we couldn't let go. On the day that came back to me, linked by filaments of sense memory to that long-ago day in Michigan, I had gotten terribly drunk in the afternoon, mixing Liebfraumilch wine with amphetamines and then orange juice laced with a small bottle of paregoric, a tincture of opium flavored with aniseed and benzoic acid. I had gone to my ex-wife's home at just about dusk, and I collapsed on the bed. She brought me icy Coca-Cola to drink, aspirins, and unfiltered Camel cigarettes, which she had to light for me, so jumpy were my hands. I slouched against the headboard, too stoned to talk. She sat beside me.

There was a sound on the other side of the door. She passed to it quickly, opened it, and there sat our daughter, Kamala, startled back from leaning against the door to hear what was going on. Kamala was four then. Her mother told her to go outside and play, that I was sick. After a few moments, I looked out into the yard where Kam was listlessly pushing herself around in circles on the swing set.

Linked by blood and illness, a six-year-old boy crouched on a landing and a four-year-old girl, alone on a swing set, circled a dead patch of earth.

In the world of cause and effect, the causes are not always so baleful and the effects are not always so lachrymose. In later years, that very conditioning that gave rise to such sorrow would give rise to joy.

I had a hard time talking to my dad when I was young. I was in fearful awe of him, in his darkness and whiskey stench. I didn't know how to say, "Pay attention, Dad." Yet, I knew he loved me. I could see it, deep in his pain-filled eyes. There was a desire there to be other than what he was and there was a longing there to know his son. Today I feel such sorrow for him, in those days of perpetual longing to connect. His heart beat with life in the presence of death.

After generations of alcoholism in my family, on both sides, I was the first to break the chains. Dad quit, too, after I did. He quit because his father never could and Dad's greatest regret was that he could never talk with his dad about his alcoholism. He didn't want me to have that regret and for the last years of his life, he was my strongest ally. His longings for love and joy were fulfilled, and mercy was realized, just before the final bell.

Here's what I believe. My father, in his failures, made possible whatever wisdom it was that enabled me to stop and to stay stopped for more than twenty years. In this also lay my conditioning and eventually my release.

When, after more than sixteen years of separation, my daughter and I were reunited, the day came when she asked if I had problems with alcohol. Her mother had told her I did and her stepfather was quick to agree. But she wanted to know on her own. Yes, I did, I told her, and she said she thought that she did as well and asked for my help. My father, myself, my daughter all linked up in one causal chain. My grandfather's failings became my father's strength and he passed them on to me.

It would be facile to assume that it could have gone some other way. I might never have gotten sober or Kamala might never have asked for help. I don't think so. One mantra I use often is, "It couldn't be any other way." Given the infinite chain of cause and effect, each outcome is inevitable. How liberating! I now know that although each outcome is inevitable, the very next one is subject to conscious action on my part. At just that moment when we see through to cause and effect, we are in the position to change the cause, our actions. We can end a lifetime of picking up the straw to snort the coke! Just don't pick up the straw to snort the coke. Generations of absent fathers, like my grandfather, my father, and me, can metamorphose into generations of fathers who are fully present.

Such was my conditioning around family secrets. They linger, I learned, when they are unspoken. I have also learned that when they are acknowledged they can be transformed, and the dead husks turn to dust and are blown away on the morning's breezes.

I learned more than secrecy as a child. Subtly—so subtly I couldn't see it—I learned the value of violence, of guns, and of hatred, especially hatred of anyone not just like me and my family. These were the 1940s and 1950s, a time before catastrophic changes that have found their fulfillment in our current social malaise, but the change was moving, just below our feet, and the signs were there for those who could see. Catastrophes are preceded by the smallest chain of mundane events, and then there comes a moment of no turning back, most often unnoticed. I remember well how I felt that coming earthquake on one sun-splashed summer day in Tennessee. My racist conditioning began to unravel on that day but the family history of secrecy forbade me from saying so.

My mother's family farm in Medon, Tennessee, was a place of simple and often harsh beauties. There was the scent of honeysuckle and manure, a sweet smell that still lingers in my deepest sense memories. I saw beginnings and endings there, in the barnyard and the stockades of cattle and sheep. There were horses, pigs, and mean, hardworking mules. I had a horse of my own, a big workhorse named Whitey, who I pictured as my cowboy mount. I would ride Whitey for hours, through this farm of fields and patches of deep woods, with its wild places and its places of careful agriculture. There was a lake, a pond, and a long stream, which meandered south through the far limits of this shimmering place. Years later, my son, Will, and I would return to this place. But that's another story, just ahead. Let's you and me stay in those earlier decades for now.

This was the 1940s and 1950s and the early 1960s, days now plasticized and stuck in often sentimental, manufactured remembrance. The rebellions of the mid-1960s were forming already, born from the chicanery and selfishness of the so-called greatest generation.

There were workers on the farm; all were black and many of them were the descendants of freed slaves. They lived in concrete block and stucco houses. I hung out with them, but was told that they were, finally, not to be trusted.

On the farther reaches of the farm, there were white sharecroppers—a mean, hard-bitten bunch—who grew meager crops and made corn whiskey in hidden stills. They sold the lightnin' in quart jars to the black workers. I was told to avoid these stringy and sun-scarred people entirely. They were the bogeymen of my childhood. There was deep racial hatred just breaking through the national soil and a beginning of a consuming-based national preoccupation with safety and social isolation. Something was coming, as something is always coming. Hide or seek and you shall find, either way, when the wind is strong enough.

I saw none of this, poking along on Whitey, his rhythmic walk melding with the deeper and unknown rhythms of the vast earth.

On one otherwise ordinary day, I helped my Great-Uncle Lacey inoculate some of the cattle. The cattle were driven into the main barn, one at a time, from the mud-sloppy corral just outside. The barn was a big place, with eight stalls and rooms for tack and for the patent medicines used on the livestock. There were barn cats and mice and kittens always underfoot.

As each animal would come in, we would drive him the length of the barn and up a small portable chute into a device that would trap his head. Then, bawling in fear and outrage, he would be inoculated with a hypodermic that looked the size of a furled umbrella. The vet would check the animal's ears and his eyes and then he would be released to trot down the ramp and into the front pen.

The barn, my world in a small place, was a closed system of dust and noise and stench and heat and fear.

It was my job, at ten years old, to get behind each animal and poke him with an electrified prod to force him into the chute. One such steer, sick with fear and virus, had explosive diarrhea, and by the time we were done with him, I was fouled with it. I had fallen several times in the hay and slick manure.

Uncle Lacey sent me up to the house, a longish walk away in the brutal, close-by sun. He told me to go around back and to ask the cook for help. She was a big black woman, ancient to me, but perhaps in her early fifties. She spent every day in the kitchen with my grandmother, cooking and canning. It was another magical enclave in a magical place.

I called to her and she came out onto the rickety, railless porch, raised on concrete blocks, where the border collies, Cam and Jack, slept. She took me out to the end of a building of linked sheds used as garages for trucks and small tractors, with one special building hung with aging, salt-crusted hams. At the spot she took me to there was always an iron cauldron over a fire, with steam rising from the simmering water. It was where she would boil laundry at the end of the day.

On this day, she grabbed a galvanized pail and filled it from the water pump by the cauldron, her strong arms pulling the water from the earth. There was a pervasive odor of wood smoke, creosote, and motor oil I can smell to this day.

She had me stand stock-still and threw bucket after bucket of water on me; first dressed and then stripped to my underwear. The cold water stung me. She picked my clothes up with a stick and lowered them into the steaming water. She told me to go take a good bath, with the big bar of Fels-Naptha soap, sickly yellow and harsh.

I bathed and then put on fresh dungarees and a shirt. I went to the big front porch and sat in a spring steel chair. I knew that, soon enough, my grandmother would appear, back from the orchard behind the house, with a tray carrying glasses of ice and bottles of Coca-Cola as she did every afternoon at five o'clock. I watched the movement of the trees. In faulty memory, I saw dust clouds as cars passed in the distance, going some unknown where else.

Grandmother brought the Cokes and my great-aunt Sadie joined us. I told them what had happened and about how the cook, whose name I can still not call up, had cleaned me off and boiled my clothes. In my ten-year-old way, I was saying how I felt cared for, in unforeseen and ugly circumstances. My grandmother laughed a bit and then said words I have never forgotten. "Well, bless her black, greasy heart."

I recoiled as something turned in my throat. I didn't say a word, but I never felt the same about my grandmother from that day.

We drank our Co'Colas. The winds moved in the trees. On the distant back road, people went places.

These are but two examples of a lifetime of conditioning, continuing to the present moment. Such conditioning causes suffering. We become attached to the "way things should be" based on this conditioning and we suffer greatly when, as is inevitable, the way things should be is not the way things are. Our most significant task can be to see things as they are and to get in synch with them. We can also refuse to see that suffering or can delude ourselves into the fatal belief that we are not suffering at all.

The suffering of refusing to see suffering is the greatest suffering of all. The refusal to see conditioning is a lethal form of conditioning. I was conditioned to be racist. I was also conditioned, at a deeper level, to detest racism. Conditioning is without distinction between good and bad; it simply is.

My understanding of who I have become, who I am, right now, in this present moment, is not a matter of intellect or of pop psychology or, especially, of pop spirituality. This under-standing asks a bitter cost and the dividends are uncertain.

Why bother? My deepest human conditioning, beyond the broken bodies of my family's slaves and beyond the hatred and fear of my Scottish ancestors, beyond even my felt kinship with the poets of ancient days, is to be happy. How can I be happy? Drugs didn't do it; marriage, no matter how sweet, didn't do it; and getting sober didn't do it either. Such outside analgesics only provided the oil to heat the crucible of awakening. There is no quick, fast-acting relief. Not crystals or pyramids or time travel or prayer said with the lips alone could do it.

So, how can I—and you—be happy?

That is the essential question if I am to live to good purpose. First, who is it who asks the questions? "Who are you?" asks Master Caterpillar who is, himself, merely a larvae in the process of becoming a moth or butterfly. Or, who knows, maybe a farm implement or a diamond ring.

In my life I am a skin bag of beginningless and endless cause and effect. Some of that conditioning has caused great suffering for me, my family, my friends, and countless others. But I have faith, based in evidence that beneath that conditioning is the un-conditioned one. To get to that one, I must peel away the condi-tioning of the slave owners, the mutineers, the drunks and failures, and that distant uncle whose Civil War rifle, with five notches on the barrel, so fascinated me as a boy, hypnotized al-ready by war. It is in becoming free of that conditioning, that endless chain of cause and effect, that I exercise my responsibility and for which I am accountable. This opportunity, this turning point, presents itself time and again, but in my life, it never presented itself more vividly as when a bunch of people I didn't know took the anesthesia away and presented me with a raw nerve in need of succor. That is not a happy state, but that one "seeing through" leads, inevitably, toward a succession of such awakenings, which, in my experience thus far, are never ending.

Freed of anesthesia, the creative mind takes over, presenting endless material to fuel the crucible of awakening.

Clearly I need to do . . . something.

Or perhaps I could just sit there.

I began the practice of daily meditation before I was a year sober. I have found it to be the most effective tool I have for undoing the conditioning. This practice brings all my strategies, born of my conditioning, right to the surface of my mind. Over time, I have seen through deeper social conditioning: that I am "supposed" to be comfortable; that to be safe is to be constantly wary and suspicious; that I have "rights." Beneath that conditioning is the deeper and more pernicious conditioning that has caused me to adjust to a deadly estrangement from the natural world, just as it is, perfect and complete. That conditioning is the most ancient of all, dating back for thousands of years.

It is in meditative inquiry that I am able to see through. It is not what we go through, after all, that is important; it is what we see through.

So, yes, the "something" to do is often nothing. Just sit there.

CHAPTER THREE

Just Sit There

"Why are we so afraid to meditate?"

The name of the man asking me this question should probably be Big John, but like all the rest of the names in this book, I'm not using his real one, just one that seems to fit.

Big John stands about six-foot-four and weighs in at about 250 pounds. His arms are garlanded with jailhouse tattoos. His graying hair hangs past his shoulders, and he has that haunting, distant stare you see in the eyes of men who have seen a lot. He favors T-shirts with the sleeves cut off, Levi's worn below his gut, and well-shined Tony Lama boots.

We were at a backyard barbeque in this small southern town where I have finally come to earth for a while. It was a muggy, hot day. There was no breeze and the air was laced with the scent of grilling meats. The live oak trees were draped with unmoving moss. There were a couple of dozen people enjoying the lazy afternoon—young children, yuppie couples (if there can be yuppies in such a delicious town), single women and men—the whole demographic stew and all of it marinated in southern manners and sweet, slow speech.

The "we" that John referred to was recovered and recovering

alcoholics. John had spent some time in prison and I had just been asked to put together a curriculum teaching meditation in prison. I didn't speak the prison language and so I had asked him about what approach to take and, as conversations will do on languid afternoons, it had spun off to the great percentage of people with the affliction of addiction and alcoholism who were behind our prison walls, and then into the whole population of people who had the problem and that small percentage who had overcome it, as John and I both had, one day at a time.

John worked as a counselor in prison and I led workshops for recovering people on the outside so we were both familiar with the Twelve Steps of Alcoholics Anonymous. We focused in on the Eleventh Step: "Sought through prayer and meditation to improve our conscious contact with God *as we understood Him,* praying only for knowledge of His will for us and the power to carry that out." John knew that I meditated and, as often happens in these conversations, he began to describe what he considered his meditative practice. It takes place mainly on the golf course or a nearby beach. I explained that my experience was rather different, involving a black cushion, a blank wall, and, initially, painful knees.

John had a lot of typical questions: "When do you find the time?" "So, it's just 'not thinking,' right?" "Don't you feel weird?" And comments of the self-conscious, "I know I really need to do it," stripe. I pointed out to him that of the practices described in the AA literature as "meditation," there are no descriptions of what is now considered to be meditation in the larger culture. The Asian forms of meditation, such as *zazen* and *vipassana,* were simply not commonly known in Western culture when those books were written. Now, these forms of meditation are fairly common thanks to intrepid Eastern teachers and their early students, here and in Asia, who began to write and talk about and, most valuably, *practice* meditation in the 1950s and then on into the 1960s when meditation became a growth industry. Meditation is still associated with austerity, discipline, self-denial, pain, and out-on-the-thin-edge weirdness. "Too weird for me" translates into "Too frightening to me," ultimately translating into the ego saying, "Do this and my gig is up!"

John and I talked on, as the air cooled a bit. The kids started to burn out and everyone made fervent but secret vows of vegetarianism and exercise just on the horizon. Probably tomorrow. Monday for sure.

Big John clearly knew that what he did wasn't meditation. But I fear I didn't create much enthusiasm with my samurai tales of sitting still and silent for hours on end; of black robes and incense and shouting teachers with thin oak wands hitting your shoulders. His hesitancy and my boasting aside, we managed to get to that crucial question: "Why are we so afraid to meditate?"

"Afraid."

There was a penetrating honesty in that word *afraid,* which opened up a deep inquiry for me. John didn't question, finally, the time it took, or the method, or the fallacy of "not thinking." He went right to the root of why so few people, alcoholics or not, accept this wondrous, free gift. We're afraid of it. And we don't know why.

So, thanks, John. Here's your answer. Sit back, relax, prop your boots up and turn off, tune in, come home.

A few days after this conversation, I was having coffee with

Bill, a friend who is a tai chi master and had been teaching, and continually learning, this particular art for over twenty years. Bill does not fit your image of a tai chi master. He is a big man, over six feet tall and muscular. He was a bass player in a rock and roll band until he got the message that the life of drugs, sex, and rock and roll was better left behind him. He practiced yoga for several years and then moved on to tai chi, studying with the great masters. Tai chi is deeply rooted in both Zen practice and, deeper yet, in the ancient Chinese spiritual tradition of Taoism. We will get to Taoism just ahead in my consideration of the deepest roots of addiction, the primal wound of estrangement from the world as it is. Here is a quick pointer at what is to come, as this is appropriate when we consider meditation as well. Taoism is matrilineal, earth-centered, and based in emphasis on the yin energy, the spirit of low places. Taoism survived the destructive energy of the Iron Age and rests quietly amongst us even now, in just those low places, where still waters abound.

In meditation and mindfulness practice, we are able to enter that fertile valley and see our conditioning face to face.

I asked Bill the question that Big John had asked me: "Why are we so afraid to meditate?"

"Because we think it will kill us."

"Kill *us*?"

"Kill the ego."

He had it right. I know he did because that was what I thought too.

The minute we hit the cushion, or for that matter, from my painful personal experience, the minute we sign on to study tai chi, the ego goes into full alert. All battle stations are manned.

Every bit of conditioning and every strategy devised over the millennia it took to create this ego is called into play. No wonder that I and many of my cohorts felt that reality was best left to those who couldn't handle drugs.

"Too weird."

"My mind just won't shut up. Meditation is not for my busy mind."

"I can't."

"This (whatever it happens to be) is not meditation."

"Navel-gazing slackers, every one of them!"

"Republicans (or Democrats or Christians or Jews or anarchists or Muslims or, hell, Tennesseans) don't meditate. Period."

"Hey, it's for Buddhists."

Let's stop for a minute and look at that last one before we allow the ego to hijack our conversation.

Meditation is *not* a Buddhist practice. It predates Buddhism but was used by the Buddha and incorporated into Buddhist practice. Most Buddhist practice includes meditation and, indeed, the word *Zen* is from the Chinese word *chan,* which is from the Sanskrit word *dhyana,* which means "meditation." However, no less imminent an authority than the Buddhist scholar Robert Thurman has said that we must take the Buddhism out of meditation. The impulse to silence, introspection, self-examination, and transcendence is an ancient one. We are hardwired to be still and quiet.

The process of mindfulness and meditation is personal transformation. Mindfulness meditation is simply the art and practice of paying attention to your life right now, right here. Mindfulness practice happens on the cushion, in meditation, and in the comings and goings of daily life. Mindfulness is an energy, which heightens awareness and enables insight and wisdom. In mindfulness, we are aware of the present moment and our experience of it. It is an ancient practice and one that offers personal and global healing. This is the truth. We are only human, and we might as well do it as wholly and exuberantly as we can.

Personal transformation is not the *goal* of mindfulness meditation; it is the process itself that is transformation. The process of the Twelve Steps, for example, or of any of the myriad journeys from addiction to freedom, from power to love, is transformation as well, and in the same sense that meditation and transformation or, better, enlightenment, are the same thing.

Although a form of meditation, sitting quietly and following the breath, can calm the mind and body and is a useful tool in times of stress and anxiety, mindfulness meditation with its focus on watching the mind is far different. The Zen monk Claude AnShin Thomas told a group in Gainesville, Florida, that if they wanted to get into meditation for stress reduction, they were quite possibly in a lot of trouble. He said about meditation, "It's like sitting on a time bomb." Make no mistake, stress reduction (better called *equanimity* for our purposes) is the inevitable result of meditation. For many people, that is quite sufficient! But the willingness to throw yourself right into the center of your life, right smack dab in the middle of the soup, is a wonderful commitment. And it never ends.

The object of meditation is the study of the mind. We observe the troublemaker.

It has been our habit to do with the mind what we do with

all phenomena: we categorize and judge it. We make an active flow of thoughts, feelings, and sensations into a separate thing. We try to make the fluid, static. And often we treat it as an enemy. We say, "It's all in my mind," which, while true to a degree, makes the mind into a separate thing with concrete qualities. As we progress in meditation and mindfulness practice, we see the mind for what it is: insubstantial and neutral. It simply reflects. This "mind" is what Buddhists call the "small mind" because it limits us to the fantasies created by our desires and dreams. If we persist in our study of the mind through meditation, eventually it falls apart and we find that underneath that never-ending flow of thoughts, images, and chatter is a radical quietness, which is radiant, pure, and immense.

This ultimate nature of mind is called "big mind" since it includes the entire world, not just our ego. This realization can have profound transformational effects: through it we find that we can reduce the negative habits of the mind—greed, anger, fear, aversion, and the like—and that we can increase the positive habits of the mind, such as love, joy, compassion, and equanimity. Neither anger nor joy is inherently in the mind. They are added. They arise and they fall away, like the breath. This is a very important understanding. With time and constancy and the light of pure awareness, the mind can be trained and the suffering falls away.

The mind is the horse we are riding, not a horse that is riding us. There is a wonderful hand scroll from the Yuan Dynasty called *Six Horses*. One of these panels has been reproduced on a greeting card. I have framed it and put it on my desk. It is a simple painting of a man riding a horse. It is a beautiful and peaceful painting in shades of tan, gray, brown, and yellow with a startling splash of red. When I look at it, I am reminded of the one thing I can control: my mind. There is one thing over which I am not powerless: my mind.

The small mind, which is impermanent, tells us that other things, other constructs, are permanent. We need to see the world as predictable and controllable. There is a desperate longing for safety and comfort, which has the opposite effect of creating a prison. In our addiction, we were perfectionists, certain that if we got just the right combination of drugs, or drinks, or love, or work, or donuts, everything "would be all right." As we close our doors and lock our gates, we are making ourselves unhappy in the pursuit of happiness. We shut down into isolation, trying to hold everything in place. In reality, the mark of all people, places, and things is impermanence. Like the breath, nothing lasts. Like the breath, everything changes. When I try to hold on to something, it is like holding my breath. I am interrupting the order of arising and falling away.

As we learn to meditate and practice mindfulness, we begin to see our stories about people and places and things as they really are: mind things as insubstantial as spun sugar.

In recovery from addiction, and in the life after recovery, we walk the path through the dangerous "mind-field" with an attitude of self-acceptance and self-care. The Sanskrit word *maitri* means "kindness" or "loving-kindness." But a basic understanding is necessary as we begin this profound practice of just sitting upright and still in the midst of things—whether we consider them "good" or "bad" or any other judging idea.

Metta practice is the practice of offering loving-kindness to yourself, to others, and to all beings. It is an ancient and fruitful practice. It is also important to note at this point that it is a non-theistic practice. This does not mean that there is any assumed position about the existence or nonexistence of God. It is about relieving suffering, our own and others'. It means only that our choices are exclusively our own. What we find beneficial and what we find not beneficial is based right here, within us. As we practice meditation we are learning to be loving and gentle. As we continue this practice, we can begin to understand how it feels to be loved and to be treated with kindness. We will know what true happiness is and once we have had this experience for ourselves, we will want it for everyone.

If we wish to be among gentle people, then we must learn to be gentle. If we are going to be gentle toward others, we must learn to be gentle toward ourselves. When you learn to love yourself, you learn to love everybody as you do yourself.

The gentle art of meditation is also the *other* choice when we are pushed right to the edge of our own intolerance of the situations of our lives. It is not the choice we are aware of. The usual and quite human choice is to find a way to run away from the edge. We have many ways to run away. We find ways to dull the discomfort. Chocolate cake is a good one. Love. Whiskey. Work. "Entertainment" is a popular choice today.

It is right here at the thin edge of our tolerance for our raw experience that the addictions show up. It is right here that we look, again, outside of ourselves for some way out of our discomfort.

The core addiction is to our illusory identity: to the "self," separate and alone. We are hopelessly addicted to the idea of "I" or "me." It is also right here, on the edge of our discomfort, that we can take the opportunity to enter fully and lovingly into the reality of our lives. Here we can renounce the limited life of distraction, denial, and threadbare safety and choose to tumble heedlessly and freely into the human soup. Pepper and all.

The elements of mindfulness exist in most religious traditions. In the Eastern traditions, mindfulness is the practice of being fully alert to the present moment. In Western traditions, it is a matter of being attentive to the divine in every moment. This is the intersection of the worlds of the poet Gerard Manley Hopkins and Basho, the master of the haiku. Right here, right now is the sacred moment. Right here, right now is the ordinary moment. In starting mindfulness practice, we are beginning the celebration of the ordinary. It begins, the simple practice, exactly as all of our lives begin: with a breath. Everything rises, everything falls away. The breath arises, the breath falls away. From the beginning of the journey to love, we will practice meditation by following the breath. This is also mindfulness practice. Now we can take it off the pillow, out of the corner of the room, or out of the soft spot in the backyard and into our lives.

Simply breathing and noticing our surroundings is not a state we are accustomed to. Although the addiction to alcohol or other drugs is behind us now, the habit of running away from the present moment is well entrenched. In the shower, we think about eating breakfast, we think about getting to work, we think about getting away from work, or the meeting we will have, or whether this is the very day that we will be fired, and then our family will soon enough be homeless and the children taken away by welfare, and the prophecies of those who hated us will come true.

Monkey mind. Inhabiting the past and the future. Missing the present moment. As we get into the habit of simply breathing and noticing the tricks of the mind, we will begin to develop constancy. This is a tricky time. Many of us wish to develop more patience and tolerance through mindfulness practice, but it is really constancy that we need. To be tolerant of someone is to be impatient. To be patient is to be intolerant. It is not acceptance and tolerance that are the goal here. When you are tolerating someone or being patient with him or her, you are in a position of judgment. One fruit of mindfulness practice is the *nonjudgmental witness.* "Grant me the serenity to accept" could be "grant me the spirit, the breath, the constancy, to accept." We learn to accept others and ourselves, exactly as we are. There is a sense of intimate involvement with every aspect of our lives and every person in our lives without judgment. This is extraordinarily difficult. So it is time to start. In appendix 2 at the back of this book are specific suggestions as to the "how-to" of meditation and mindfulness practice.

In the winter of 2003/2004, I stopped meditating and began to take the spiritual path for granted. I went to places in my mind that were not safe. I can't claim that such behavior was at cause for what was to come, but I think it helped.

I am reminded now of T-shirts I made for my friend Lenny and myself in 1985. The slogan on the front was "Take my advice. I'm not using it."

CHAPTER FOUR

In the Realm of the Wraiths

At three in the morning, I am defenseless. It is then, but not only then, that the wraiths will appear, whispering with voices as thin and sinister as straight razors. The wraith is the skillful confabulator who weaves stories from shards of memory, filling in the spaces where memory fails or, the truth unknown, with the most menacing of lies.

They are cunning and wear clever disguises. Their wit is sharp, their stories convincing, their aim is unerringly at the softest part of us. They can bring breathtaking gifts. In my case, the wraiths ushered in a sacred catastrophe for which I finally became grateful.

I make no contribution here to the culture of "feel good" and "positive thinking," which only blunts the senses to the feelings of others, creating an atmosphere of narcissism and offering precious little opportunity for personal responsibility or atonement. This story is a look at the mindscape of profound and all-too-conscious despair, and at the structure and power of meekness, beneath conscious knowing.

My wraiths entered through my ego, the easiest way in. I mistook a spiritual experience for a spiritual awakening and, further, I forgot that a spiritual awakening is not the end of something, but the beginning.

In late November of 2003 a friend invited me to come and see a statue of the Buddha of the future, Maitreya Buddha, which was then on tour to raise funds for a 500-foot statue to be erected in India. At the end of a social evening, looking at this statue and its attendant smaller statues of various Buddhist saints, I was asked to stay behind for a blessing by the Lama who was touring with this statue. I did so. The Lama moved around the small circle of people who had stayed behind. He carried a small chalice that contained the "relics" of Shakyamuni Buddha, the historical Buddha, and touched each person, in turn, on the top of the head with the chalice. In the course of that blessing, I felt a surge of power and of connection to the earth that was unique in my experience. What I would not know for many months to come is that everything that had gotten stuck in my psyche had been cut loose.

So uncertain am I, however, that I can see it is also quite possible that that experience had nothing to do with what was to come. I know only that it fed my spiritual arrogance, leaving me vulnerable in my assurance.

I recalled that six years before this event I had found a way of praying that was comfortable to me and out of the comfort came a prayer that I said with full fervor and intention. The prayer was this: "May I be changed in ways I cannot possibly imagine." I think that might have been a reckless prayer. On this night, I thought it had been answered. Maybe it was.

That November evening, after the blessing, I hopped on my bike and rode around Gainesville for a while. I ate some Krispy

Kremes at one of the original Krispy Kreme stores. I went home. Life went on. I felt elated. Beware elation, for it is as dangerous as depression and far more cunning. Just beneath the surface there was movement of which I was unaware that would take me to a place I had only dreamt of before in recurrent nightmares as a child.

In that dreamtime, I was the sole visitor in a hospital ward for those who had been profoundly injured. I had this dream for many years, well into my adult life, but each time I dreamt it, I was the age I was at the time I dreamt it first. I dreamt it first in an awful year for my family and an especially awful year for me, filled with fear and, most important, uncertainty. It was 1949 and I was a sickly seven-year-old, plagued by chronic ear infections and fevers and unable to attend school for more than a month in the entire school year.

In this dream ward, each being was a long, glistening, living nerve. That was all that was left of them after whatever horrors they had experienced. Everything had been stripped away, leaving only this tissue. They were bodiless but sentient. Each of them lay in a vat of some unknown liquid and the vats were bathed in sickly green light. They were in constant and ruthless pain. They screamed in thin, warbling high notes. Such was my dream. I had not dreamt it in many years, but it was with me until I was in my mid-thirties.

By that night in 2003, I had become vulnerable after many years of being free of chemicals and of daily meditative spiritual practice. I knew in my mind that the spiritual life is not a comfortable one, but I had not experienced that truth. To become truly vulnerable is a great gift but it can lead to places that are perilous. Vulnerability can lead to the gift of the truth. The dawning of truth is like no other, in my experience. The inner landscape is raw, at first, and the light is vicious.

I cannot possibly say with any assurance at all what convergence of events led to my night of the soul. I have some ideas about it, but ideas here are useless. There were precipitating events for which my experience with the Buddha's relics had perhaps prepared the ground, but there were many more causes and many more effects of which I have no knowledge at all and never will.

The important cautionary story here is the one of the relics. There is an old Zen saying that captures it perfectly: "Don't mistake a fisheye for a pearl."

I am also certain that what happened could not have been any other way. Millions of vectors of cause and effect converged and I was plummeted into a spiral tunnel downward that only today I can see as a birth canal.

The greatest and most transformative trials are not the ones we construct. Working the Twelve Steps is still intentional, as much as it is often feared. As spooky as seated meditation can be, it is still chosen and there is some sense of control. The onset of the greatest transformations is always unbidden and unexpected. This is the sacred catastrophe.

By the beginning of March 2004, I was in a state of anxious despair of a proportion I could not have imagined. I was so afraid of the outside world that I couldn't leave my house. I slept only fitfully. I couldn't eat but forced myself to choke something down each day.

The walls of my rooms, which I had painted in tropical

tones, became garish and threatening. I wrote long and incoherent letters to friends, analyzing, analyzing, and analyzing this state. I was afraid. I hated. I was living in the realm of the wraiths. From fear comes anger, from anger comes hate, and from hate comes suffering. I was without hope, without faith, without dreams. As in those prescient childhood dreams, I was stripped raw.

The wraiths had their way with me, whispering lies. Here is an important understanding: the wraiths are always wrong. I knew that and, at times, I took comfort in it.

Everything I had relied on for years failed me. My friends—the ones who could stand to be around me—tried to help. Two of them, Feral Willcox and John Hall, did help. But it was not enough. The community of recovery failed; my meditation practice failed; my thinking and analyzing failed. My doctor offered to prescribe antidepressants and I refused them. Somehow I began to see that I had to mount this dragon and let it run.

I went to therapy, briefly, when I was finally able to leave the house for an hour or two. After three weeks of this, I saw that therapy was not the answer here. I told my therapist that this was not a psychological crisis. So-called "inner-child work," often an indulgence and sometimes a help, was of no use. Behavior modification was of no use. The intellectual therapeutic approach, in which I was encouraged to pathologize my behavior and the behavior of others, failed. I told my therapist that what I had been thrown into was soul work, in the midst of a spiritual crisis, and that such work can only be done alone. She agreed.

No more pathology, no more meditative inquiry, no prayer,

no faiths, no community, no science, no steps, no more God, no Buddha, no saints, no ghosts or angels supported me.

It was the end of certainty. This foul desire for certainty is one of the greatest causes of suffering. It is an addiction like few others, causing untold misery in families, in communities, in nations, and in the world itself. My years of drug addiction were a relentless longing for certainty and perfection. I want, I want, I want to be comfortable and secure in some precise way that only I can understand and yet, that nothing—absolutely nothing, no matter how perfectly configured—can offer.

There was no certainty of process or outcome left. I was helpless.

That was the first blessing.

For weeks after leaving the therapist, I rode the dragon. In Tibetan Buddhist iconography the dragon is symbolic of great courage and awakening and appears in springtime. It was springtime, but I had no courage and had no thought of awakening. I was wild with fears I could not name. Underneath my skin, I trembled. My behavior became increasingly erratic. I wrote more loopy letters to old friends. I apologized, by mail, to people who I hadn't hurt; people who, in fact, had hurt me. I still regret two of those letters.

The turning point, like the catastrophe, came unexpectedly and unbidden.

On a morning in early April, I lay down on the floor of my kitchen, just to have something to hold on to. I calmed my mind as best I could on the cool tiles. I knew, without doubt, the truth, in a turning moment of great clarity and remarkable equanimity.

"If this goes on much longer, I can kill myself."

That was the second blessing.

In a Thanatos-oriented culture, suicide is the final drug of choice. What are addictions of any sort if not slow suicide? I saw that suicide was my preferred drug then and, at a level just above the unconscious, it had always been there, offering relief from pain. In order to kill the part that hurt, I had to kill my self. My death would bring the final oblivion, the cessation of suffering and pain. Nothing. Forever.

The next thought, entirely intuitive, after I had absorbed the first, was the clear knowing that I would not kill myself. Now I truly had nothing left, nowhere else to go. I was at dead center and completely helpless. I was at dead center and totally free. There was nothing left to lose.

I had meekly surrendered. I had not made a decision based on considerations and weighing of alternatives. This surrender was at a cellular level.

Over the next weeks and months, I followed where a new and surprisingly powerful sense of intuition led me. I reread classic spiritual literature like the *Bhagavad Gita* and the *I Ching*. I began studying the Bible and recovery-related literature with a kind and gentle man named Papa John. He came to my home, like clockwork, on Wednesday afternoons. We looked at primary sources, at commentaries and abstracts, in an atmosphere of love. At his urging, every night for a month I read the first letter of Paul to the Corinthians, chapter thirteen. In the ultimate lines of that verse I read, "But now faith, hope, love abide these three, but the greatest of these is love."

In my dark night, I had abandoned hope and I had given no

thought, none at all, to love, and yet through some ineffable grace I had fallen, at last, into love.

That was the third and, for this part of the journey, the final blessing.

Here are verses four through seven of 1 Corinthians.

"Love is patient, love is kind and is not jealous; love does not brag and is not arrogant; does not act unbecomingly; it does not seek its own, is not provoked, does not take into account a wrong suffered, does not rejoice in unrighteousness; bears all things, believes all things, endures all things." The chapter continues with brilliant restatements of these themes, ending in the majestic thirteenth verse, quoted here.

I cannot urge you strongly enough to read verses four through thirteen of the thirteenth chapter of 1 Corinthians as I did, last thing at night, and with your entire body and mind.

This majestic recitation of what love is and is not, is a description of meekness. *Meek* is not a word one hears often, except perhaps from Sunday pulpits and then only quoted, most often from the Beatitudes. I hope that we can begin to use this word again, with its connotations of gentleness and kindness and a wisdom that dismisses pain and elation equally. The old Taoists would get it, I'm sure, and maybe some of the Ch'an masters of China, many centuries before Paul ever wrote a word.

To be meek, I flatter myself to think Lao Tzu might feel, is to be like water, content with the low places that people disdain, nourishing all without intending to do so. To be meek is to be that which, constant in its course, wears away every obstacle.

It was love that led me beside still waters.

If you are skeptical, as I was, you may do as I did. Read through the Twelve Steps of Alcoholics Anonymous and replace the word *God* everywhere it appears with the word *love*. I found that love is the power greater than myself.

I had awakened to love, in love, and by love's grace. This was only the beginning. The great joy and the great promise of the spiritual life, I had finally seen, is that it has no ending.

Over the next few weeks I began to return to life, or better, to begin anew. We must always be beginning, after all, if we don't want to get stuck.

I began reading the great poets of China and Japan once more. The books of the poems of Li Po, Po Chu-I, Tu Fu, Cold Mountain, Pickup, Stonehouse, T'ao Ch'ien, and anthologies with yet more of the greats littered my floors. I read Westerners as well: Wallace Stevens, T. S. Eliot, Sharon Olds, Mary Oliver, and Gary Snyder.

Love redeemed me, and poetry—love's greatest vehicle— restored me.

I had suffered from a love and poetry deficit.

The previous year while reading T'ao Ch'ien I had found the following poem. It stuck with me and during this joyous orgy of reading, I sought it out again.

People praise Yen's benevolence, say
Jung mastered the Way. So often empty,

one died young. Always hungry, the other
lived to a ripe old age. Their names

outlived death, but they eked out such
haggard lives. And renown means nothing

once we're dead and gone. Simple-hearted
contentment—it's all that matters.

We coddle thousand-gold selves, but
we're only guests; change soon takes

our treasure. Why not naked burial?
People need to get beyond old ideas.

T'AO CH'IEN,

TRANSLATED BY DAVID HINTON

That one poem and its central single phrase, "simple-hearted
contentment" pointed the way to a road in the distance with an
uncertain destination, if any at all, that I was destined to walk,
at last.

I read what scant information is available about T'ao Ch'ien.
His dates are 365–427 CE. He was born into a tumultuous time
of corruption and war and barbarian invasions. He longed to
return to his family farm, but for years he worked as a func-
tionary in government service. He was a Taoist and a dedicated
Confucian as well. He left government service at age thirty-nine
and, after several moves and false starts, he settled, in the year
402, into the life of a recluse farmer, a hermit. This was not some
romantic ideal, familiar to some of us who went "back to the

land" in the 1960s only to take all of our romantic notions and desire for comfort with us. T'ao Ch'ien moved to a farm in order to dwell in "the great transformation," the rhythms of the earth and the seasons in which all that happens is artless and spontaneous, the turning of the great engine, the Tao.

I found kinship with this man, not in his achievements certainly, but in his longings. His influence had only begun. My relationship to this man began to shine a light on additional bits of hitherto hidden directions home.

In the late summer of 2004, my son, Will, and I took a trip up Highway 61, the legendary Blues Highway, which runs through the Mississippi Delta, my mother's original home. We visited every blues site we could find and attended a blues festival in Clarksdale, the town where it is said that blues great Robert Johnson had sold his soul to the devil in exchange for guitar skills at the Crossroads. Will and I found a crossroads we thought was the "real" one and I knelt there and scooped up some Mississippi soil and put it in the leather mojo bag that hung from my belt.

The skilled novelist Ace Atkins refers to these great blues singers as "The Zen Poets of Mississippi." Amen.

We found the grave of Charlie Patton, the man many consider to be the first great blues guitarist. The grave, in a field behind a church in Holly Crossing with the vast horizons of the delta stretching in every direction, is a simple one. Over the years, determined pilgrims have left guitar picks, capos, and spare change there for this man. We stood in silence for long minutes in the dead hot air. We were on our way home.

Two days later, we were in Memphis, the home of another blues singer whose life turned out rather different from Charlie Patton's. We had thought about going to his home, Graceland, thus living out a Paul Simon song, but the sad hordes of Elvis worshipers on Beale Street sobered us up. We skipped Graceland, content with the stark beauty of Patton's grave and legend.

By the next afternoon, we were in Medon, Tennessee, my childhood equivalent of T'ao Ch'ien's farm on the northwest side of Lu Mountain, centuries before. The present owner of the farm has left the "home place" buildings as they were, only cleaning them up and repairing them as needed. In this epicenter of my childhood, Will told me that he understood why I had wandered so far in my life. He reckoned I was used to horizons and simplicity and had searched for that home all of my life. I think so, but I also believe he was describing himself as well. He had connected with his ancestors and the earth in which they lay buried. He had connected to all the ancestors, unseen, and the earth as it is.

Yes, he had it right—for me, for him, and for you. Is that home in Medon or Lu Mountain or is it somewhere we've missed? It's all of those, *concretized* in the place I called home. This was the first hint to me that the home we miss is this great earth that we were wrenched from long ago and from which we have been estranged ever since.

I was a child in Medon and as a child I lived in a blissful, erotic connection with the natural world. Deeply encoded bonds to the ancient times were everywhere enriched by water, fire, and earth. In this matrix, I had lived by my senses and upon my return from the night of the soul, years later and just months before this moment Will and I shared, I had returned to my senses.

Coda: During the springtime days of darkness I had traveled to Austin, Texas, to spend time with two close friends: Pat, who lives in the Hill Country there, and Elene, who lives in Minnesota and with whom I have led meditation workshops. One night, as Pat played the piano and Elene and I drummed along, Elene remembered a prayer she had learned many years before. During a break, sensing that I was hurting, she told it to me. I prayed it that night and did so for the rest of that year. Here is the prayer: ✓ "Give me the heart of a child, and the awesome courage to live that out."

I think this prayer is being answered, incrementally and gently. One journey had ended and another, inevitably, had begun.

CHAPTER FIVE

Something's Happening Here

Dug under earth's crust for drugs
to make me immortal.
Turned mountains to ash hunting alchemical ore.
Then followed rivers
back to their source;
groveled, swallowed pride,
tried to get favor with kings.
Hooked on spells
Hung up on weird arts
I wandered the charnel grounds—
but never shed craving—
never obtained a single pierced
cowrie shell.

BHARTRIHARI (INDIA, SEVENTH CENTURY)

Bhartrihari was known principally as a grammarian although such works as this poem would stick him squarely in the pantheon of Buddhist philosophers. As I struggled through his works, unsuccessfully, I was reminded of a phrase a critic once used, predicting playfully what the great playwright Samuel

Beckett was up to. He reckoned that one day, Mr. Beckett would write a play of "one fragrant monosyllable." That is a coy and reasonable idea, given Beckett's increasingly spare opus. In fact, Bhartrihari was searching for that one primal sound. According to the Internet Encyclopedia of Philosophy, "His thought may be characterized as part of the *shabdadvaita* (word monistic) school of thought, which asserts that cognition and language at an ultimate level are ontologically identical concepts that refer to one supreme reality, Brahman."

I was lost in these words, so I asked for help.

I found a congenial and anonymous ScholarGhost deep in the Internet. We were able to get beyond the work of Bhartrihari and return to the inquiry that put us together, in cyberland, in the first place. "What's a pierced cowrie shell and what is the story of this poem?" My Ghost would not let me make the usual detour into my head, entranced by history rather than living in at least the same neighborhood as my heart. Returned to heart-knowing, we had an interesting colloquy about these few words of the Indian sage. We agreed that this was not so much a description of Bhartrihari's life as a description only of his youth and, in fact, an excellent description of universal youthful folly.

This fragment of a poem by him struck me as completely Buddhist when I read it, particularly in the phrase "never shed craving." In my own folly I failed, for two years, to understand why I was drawn to it. I had come across it, by accident, on the Internet. I stuck it up on the bulletin board in my office to be used, someday, in *Silver Tea,* my online letter to my son. I saw this poem as a succinct explanation of what many other people do in their eagerness to know that they are alive. As is often the

case, I find it easy to see what others do and need and to understand what demons drive them. Rarely have I been able to accept
such signposts as being on my path as well. It was only after a
profound and piercing shamanic experience in the Golfo Dulce
and the rain forest of Costa Rica that I had the internal mecha-
nism to deal dispassionately with the subtler forms of coincidence as they reflect my own life.

Life is richer in coincidence than in meaning.

When I notice a flower blooming at the base of a live oak
outside my writing room window, it has no meaning. It's a
flower in an unexpected place, nothing more. If I have read
about that particular flower in one of my Florida natural history
books recently, then the coincidence is interesting, but easily dismissed. If the flower is a Turk's-cap lily, a common enough
flower that I had not previously known the name of and which
is a very showy plant indeed, with colors I associate with Tibet,
Nepal, and Bhutan, I will make a leap, if I am paying attention.
Turk's-cap! How exotic and how endowed with a funky Florida
gris-gris that casts fog around the present place and moment and
beckons to farther places and times. Within moments I will be
immersed in memories of treks in that part of the world, and
then possibly onward to thoughts of my soul friend Masha, who
I met in Bhutan years ago. At that point I might be reminded of
what it is like to love and to be loved, with no expectation, no
clinging. The event, the unexpected appearance of the flower,
has been given meaning, by me alone, and in this case could well
provide solace on a day of internal loneliness.

But let me add one more supposition here.

What if, on the day of the magical appearance of that lily, I was searching for a way to describe meaningful coincidence in a way that would be transparent and precise? What if my mind was open to being flirted with by random happenings and my neural pathways were clear enough to make jumps beyond reason, extending into what might seem to be magic? What if, that is, I was at one with my environment and entirely teachable?

And what if I sat down at my typewriter and told you about it? We would have formed a mini-community of linked stories, based in spontaneous occurrences, and perhaps understand each other better. A conspiracy of meaning.

That's what happened, of course, in real time this very day.

The coincidences were mere; the meaning I gave them was useful.

There is no meaning to any occurrence, person, place, or thing other than the meaning I give it. There are links of co-incidence that are forged in my own internal conditioning and prejudices that have the power to either deceive or enlighten.

It was the open mind of inquiry, informed only with a question, quickly forgotten but churning away nonetheless, and with no assumptions of what I might find, that brought together those events in meaning. Did I do it? Did I bring those events to-gether or did I simply notice the useful spikes of coincidence that pointed to a gate I needed to go through? I think the latter is what's true.

You can do it. Just ask a question, swallow it whole, and then pay attention to what's right in front of you. Don't get eager.

So what of the Bhartrihari poem?

I said in the introduction that when I began to write this book, I was troubled as to what direction it might take and what

I "should" and "should not" write about. I have long been one who doesn't much care for the "drunkalogue," that harrowing tale of jails and teeth falling out and guns and endless similar encounters with the shaman-turned-evil. I feel that such stories could have two ill effects. The first is that they might seem perversely glamorous and inviting to the TV generation, dulled to reality and immersed in just such stories, where only the bad guys die. The second is that it might be seen that others must go where I went and, further, could go there and return safely, as I did.

These descriptions of the diseased soul that I've told here in this book and any yet ahead aren't glamorous unless I think they are. I don't think they are. Because they aren't. Simple. As to the second hesitation: you don't have to go there and might not come back if you do. And it's all a dismal waste of time!

Don't be fooled. I offer these images of separation because they are the truth and because they point to quicksand I hope that others won't step into. Stories of heaven are boring; tales of hell excite us. But not if we've been in hell. At that point, and on the return, it is the portrayals of heaven that buoy us up. The portrayals of hell are mere reminders of the grace and the power of the present, heavenly moment.

But without some binding narrative—some yin and yang, some contrast, and some deeper intuition of the whole pointed to by the parts—they are only stories, amusing or scary by turn without a larger and useful harmony.

Stories work better when the storyteller is able to see a theme, a persistent and vivid one. Random tales of self-slaughter get attention and can be good teachers, but it's more useful to look closely for the micro-thread that unites and informs them all.

The poem, I saw, was an accurate map of my own wanderings. From army officer in 1966 to patchouli-drenched stoner in 1967; from a child of privilege and southern gentility to a wastrel in a shack in the Mexican desert in a span of two years in the early 1960s—I had played all of these parts and more.

Here is a partial list of the drugs I have used: lysergic acid diethylamide (LSD), mescaline, psilocybin, peyote, dimethyl-tryptamine (DMT), ayahuasca, codeine, methamphetamine (most memorably mixed with LSD and snorted on the night of the first moon landing), Benzedrine, Dexedrine, cocaine, opium, marijuana, hashish, Percodan, paregoric, belladonna, Valium, Xanax, Ativan, Serax, Librium, Dalmane, and that charming couple just down the block, ethyl and methyl alcohol.

I didn't much care for the marijuana.

My gut and brain formed a lethal cornucopia.

Why?

Here are some of the conventional explanations.

SPIRITS

Here is part of a letter from the great Swiss psychoanalyst Carl Jung to AA cofounder Bill Wilson, concerning a man who had become a member of AA after "failing" in treatment with Dr. Jung.

Dear Mr. W.,

Your letter has been very welcome indeed.

. . . [Rowland H.'s] craving for alcohol was the equivalent, on a low level, of the spiritual thirst of our being for

wholeness, expressed in medieval language: the union with God . . .

You see, "alcohol" in Latin is "spiritus" and you use the same word for the highest religious experience as well as for the most depraving poison. The helpful formula therefore is: spiritus contra spiritum.

Thanking you again for your kind letter . . .

C. G. Jung

These excerpted sentences are often quoted in the literature of recovery. They offer a compelling explanation of the spiritual path concretized in a monotonous solitude. Was my drunkenness and addiction a low-grade equivalent of a spiritual search? *Equivalent* is a powerful word. According to the dictionary it means equal to; having the same weight, effect, or value; or "meaning." If I am to follow Dr. Jung in his reasoning, I have to say that the "meaning" of my addiction was that I was, below consciousness, engaged in a spiritual venture. This point of view can be remarkably persuasive.

Like the Fool in the tarot deck, I set out empty and naive, and through a series of adventures and encounters with the gods, I was, like Jason, finally brought into the presence of the Golden Fleece or the Cup of Wisdom. In the real world I endured near-death experiences, time after time, pierced by the swords of my own folly and led astray by one trickster after another. I drank alcohol on top of the drug Antabuse on two occasions. I was once carried into an emergency room in Chicago with IVs in both arms and the back of one hand, with a pulse rate over 150, unable to hear over the roaring of my blood in my ears. That excursion was the inevitable outcome of spending two weeks on Islamorada, in the Florida Keys, doing cocaine in order to stop drinking.

I had wandered into churches, mosques, synagogues, temples, and zendos seeking comfort and release. I had prayed and I had meditated. I had attached myself to ballroom gurus, actually befriending one of the most charismatic of the crew. Was I, in fact, searching for God?

The story of Jason and the Argonauts certainly works, but my romantic preference—and I suspect that all such choices are in fact romantic—is to see myself as Indiana Jones in the final movie of that trilogy, reunited with the father, as I was, and making the simple, clear choice of the Holy Grail, inconspicuously placed amongst more glittering choices. (Indiana had the really neat hat, and the whip—for heaven's sake, the whip!) Indiana, after all, was just looking for "stuff" and happened to fall upon spirit.

An interesting choice, this hero's journey. It is valid and useful. But it is not, I now see, my own.

I have read many books written by people who are clearly spiritually adept and persuasive, in which they speak of a desire, born in childhood, to know God, acknowledged and always present. In other books I have read and in many stories I have been told in the community of recovery, I have heard the same.

Alas, I have never known such a desire. It was never God I sought. I am not a religious man, nor a superstitious one. My path has been one of the senses, rather than spirit.

If it was anything at all, this search, it was a desire to hide from the minions of God and from God himself. I did not feel that God was within me, but that demons were. I did not feel that God was outside of me, a holy thing that would save me from the very demons I saw everywhere. A pervasive awareness of despair and alienation shadowed me. I wished to build my own tower and to speak my own exclusive language.

The tower was built of hatred and greed, filled, finally, with wind and fire and spirit. Like the tower in Babel, like other towers, it would inevitably fall. I wanted all that life had to give, except those parts that made me uncomfortable or challenged my conditioned beliefs. I knew where to find escape, although I gave escape some other names.

Not God, but other more troubling illusions, informed my life.

THE SHAMAN'S WAY

In the earlier list, I mention all the psychedelic or psychotropic drugs I took. Some were synthetics, such as LSD, and others were naturally occurring, such as peyote. There are volumes of research of the spiritual efficacy of such substances. Respected academics and academic outlaws have used these "spiritual friends" and have reported convincingly on the spiritual dimensions of their experiments.

I first took LSD in 1967, the fabled "Summer of Love," while living on the Haight-Ashbury in San Francisco. In those days, stretched to weeks and to months, my hair was to my shoulders and I reeked of patchouli. I bought gallons of Red Mountain burgundy wine at a time. Back then the gallon jug cost $1.99. A British singer's ideas to the contrary, I did not wear flowers in my hair. I had a poster of the brilliant comic Lenny Bruce on one wall of my apartment and a Day-Glo poster of the White Rabbit on another. I went to the Fillmore Auditorium and the Avalon Ballroom and danced under strobe lights, the walls splashed with the moving and interpenetrating amoebas, snapshots, paisleys, mandalas, and exploding colors of light shows. I heard Hendrix and Jefferson Airplane and the Grateful Dead and a platoon of other bands and I was high all the time. I don't regret a minute of it. Now I am aware of something I couldn't see then, in my own private purple haze.

I was just wearing the uniform I had to wear to fit in and get high. Only a year previous, my uniform had been that of an infantry officer, with my airborne wings and lieutenant's bars. No difference, except in time and place and choice of drugs.

I was eager to try LSD. I had seen stories about it in media as diverse as the *Berkeley Barb* and *Life* magazine.

The night of that first trip, the India-print bedspreads on the walls of my lover's apartment became vast fields of three- and then multi-dimensional movement and color. Candle flames shed light of unknown hues in far corners of the room. When my lover and I went outside, at 3 a.m., to Balboa Park to dance in the brilliant and supernatural starlight, I knew I had found another dimension of the universe, of life itself, that I had never suspected existed. We danced and I felt every bump and curve and delicious texture of her body against mine, under silk and denim. Her smile was the smile of a person in rapture and her eyes drew me in to their spectral blues.

Back in her California Street apartment, we ate apples and blue cheese and drank wine and listened to Ravi Shankar records. We looked closely at the Day-Glo paisley paper the acid-soaked sugar cube had been packaged in. As dawn spilled over the shutters, we made love, languorously, intensely, gently, and roughly, at some moments looking deeply into each other, at others growling, primitive animals from an unknown savanna, moving together, boundaries dissolved into joy.

It was a wonderful and life-enhancing experience. My lover and I have been out of touch for many years now. I saw her once, in 1970, in a bookstore where I worked in Greenwich Village. We spoke only of current things. She turned me on to Marquez's *One Hundred Years of Solitude,* which I stole from the store that afternoon and read, in one sitting. I saw her once again, in 1987, on Lexington Avenue in New York. I was afraid to say hello.

In the years following the virgin experience, I took LSD many times, each time hoping to repeat that initial flight and always failing. I finally stopped in 1977 when I had an experience that was so frightening that I knew I could never return to those realms. I flew over San Francisco; I looked at my current lover and saw demons there. I fell, finally, into a pit at the center of the world where I met an ageless crone who would not show me her face.

I took other psychotomimetic drugs during those years after that golden summer. Most of "us" had stopped, empowered and changed by the social upheaval of those years, as dark as their later political results would be. On some of these drugs I got ill and moved on, on others I had alternating frightening and wonderful times, in a dimensionless world created from chemicals and overstimulated neural passages. On one occasion, at the home of a folk singer/balladeer, now dead for many years, in

Woodstock, New York, I ate psilocybin and spent the night outside, locked in conversation with a three-legged dog and a goat. Inside the house, a group called The Band played all night long. What did I know? I couldn't be bothered. The dog and the goat had so much more to teach me, it seemed.

This little organic psychedelic spree ended, with one reprise far ahead, shortly after the final LSD one, when I ate peyote buttons and mixed them with amphetamines and vodka, finally soiling myself in a very fine restaurant in Marin County.

I think it was the coq au vin.

As I was reaching for the bottom, in the winter of 1983/1984, I went to New Orleans and on out from there to the Bayou Teche to meet up with a conjure woman, a *Bruha*. She had lived on the bayou for over ninety years, yet had traveled to places I can still only imagine. She brewed me up some pot liquor at the end of our afternoon together and bade me drink it. This was pure belladonna, it turns out, *La Belle Dame sans Merci*. I spent the next forty-eight hours in a carnival inside my own head that mimicked successfully the wildest ones on the furthermost reaches of that bayou. That did it! Not because it scared me, although it did, but because I liked it too much.

Was this a search for transcendence? Did I share with the academics and outlaws a desire to see the face of God or to experience spiritual awakening?

No. Like many of my peers it was about drugs, sex, and rock and roll. I wanted to get as high as I could and stay that way for as long as I could. For most, the party finally ended. They moved on, found partners, began working at useful jobs, and were genuinely content with the path they had chosen. The era of drugs and sex and rock and roll passed and they wisely moved on.

I no longer had choices that I could see.

I was so isolated in my brain fever and reckless indifference to others that I never noticed they had left the room. The image I hold today of myself in my late twenties and all of my thirties is of a sad figure twirling in an empty white room to music only I could hear. It's a pathetic image but one that only instructs. There is no shame, just a deep sadness for all the harm I did while enraptured with Thanatos, the brother of Sleep and the son of Night. Thanatos is death and his image is frightful. The light of the sun god Helios searches for Thanatos in vain. I was lost from the light and never missed it.

I had lost my way home. Many did.

That's a romantic and self-serving notion and finally it's a false one. It describes me well in those wondrous and deceptive days. But it's not true. There is a way home.

Years later, I spent a weekend on an urban meditation retreat in noisy downtown Manhattan. The teacher held an open question-and-answer period toward the end of the two days of silence and inquiry. One meditator, who was, like me, a veteran of the Summer of Love, asked if drugs were an ally to meditative practice. After all, he reckoned, when the Zen Center of San Francisco was first operating, in those halcyon days, it was common for folks to show up to meditate, on those forbidding little black cushions, stoned to the eyeballs on marijuana or any of a broad selection of psychedelics that were so easily available on any street corner.

The teacher smiled, broadly. None of those enigmatic Zen

smiles for her! Without a pause, she said: "Drugs are for taking a trip. Meditation is about coming home."

The metaphors of spirit and shaman failed me, finally, many years into my sober life. There was a vanity there that I found uncomfortable. It was this excessive and self-centered pride that had fed my troubles and I don't find it useful to this day beyond its value as mere metaphor. I recall with some sorrow a moment in my early recovery when I took the woman who was to become my third ex-wife to a Fourth of July party given by and for recovering alcoholics. Pauline is not an alcoholic, although there was some suspicion that she is in a booze-soaked lineage. One person at the party took Pauline aside and told her, with compassion, that alcoholics tended to be more blessed with wisdom and insight than "earth people."

Pauline is an earth person. So am I. I have yet to meet anyone who is not. I must love my neighbor's folly as deeply as I love his awakening. Everyone suffers. Everyone can find the way out of suffering. My particular brand is not special.

The evil of addiction, in fact, rests in its banality.

Being alcoholic means that I have a skewed internal chemistry, with substantially peculiar brain and liver functions. It does not place me in a spiritual or intellectual elite, descended from elsewhere. Elsewhere was my home for many years, but I belong on this great earth and needed to find my way home.

Without a mythic or religious explanation of my particular addiction, I turned to science. The meaning-making mind was insistent, and scientism, after all, is the great secular religion of this moment.

SCIENCE

Addiction hijacks the cortex in the service
of the primordial lizard brain.

—STEVEN HYMAN, FORMER DIRECTOR,
NATIONAL INSTITUTE OF MENTAL HEALTH

All through 2004 and into the early spring of 2005, I devoured books, articles, abstracts, and conversations about the addicted brain and its cohort, the malfunctioning liver. After several months with such tomes as *Zen and the Brain* and *This Strange Illness,* I recklessly subscribed to *Science* magazine, posing as an academic to get the discounted subscription. I gave each issue, unread, to my friend John Hall. John is a psychiatrist who specializes in addictive medicine and reads quantum and classical physics to relax.

I was awash in data and confused. I asked for help.

The statement quoted above came from a long and cordial and deeply instructive conversation with my friend Dr. Stephen Mulkey. Stephen is an evolutionary ecologist of international reputation and is, by inclination, a student of the brain, the limbic system, the whole encompassing neural network that seems to run the show. Stephen is a striking man, handsome and tall, with a thick and perfect head of silver hair. At six-foot-two I still have to look up to meet his eyes. He has the look of someone who is more comfortable in wild places than on a college campus.

We sat in his living room on a brilliant spring day. Sunlight streaked the room into areas of light and deep darkness. Not one, but two monitors were processing data on the brain and its functions. We dove into it all, our own neurons and conditioned brains sorting, quantifying, and exclaiming over this load of information. Here is what I found in that jungle, with Stephen as seasoned trekker to guide me.

The brain is a place of high-speed neural conversation. It is a bio-computer of staggering complexity, which is only now being mapped and understood. (Mapped and understood by the brain, by the way! That seems to me like asking the Pentagon to evaluate its own chicanery.) Messages are sent and received, at blinding speed, in this vast network of billions of nerve cells, or neurons.

The neurons are mute; there is no yelling over the vast distances of the brain. Messengers are used. These messengers, called neurotransmitters, carry the story. The neurotransmitters are released by an excited neuron and set out to find a fit in the appropriate receptor cell. The shape and the electrical charge of the receptor determine the fit. Square peg; square hole. For our purposes, the most important neurotransmitters are dopamine, serotonin, norepinephrine, and the cowboy-sounding GABA. The first three of these guys collectively are responsible for feelings of well-being. Dopamine is feisty, increasing alertness, sexual excitement, and aggression while, paradoxically, reducing and at other times increasing compulsive behavior. Serotonin, another feel-good neurotransmitter, rocks us to sleep, reduces the aggressive behavior of the dopamine, and elevates the pain threshold. Norepinephrine is more quixotic, reducing compulsive behavior but in overdose producing anxiety, increasing the heart rate, and elevating blood pressure. The cowboy, GABA, reduces anxiety and compulsive behavior and, like serotonin, increases the pain threshold.

Soon, guided by Dr. Stephen and others, we will enter the abnormal landscape of the alcoholic brain. But there is one important and empirically valid assumption here:

There is a genetic predisposition to alcoholism.

That's old news. Right? William D. Silkworth, M.D., first posited such an explanation in the early days of Alcoholics Anonymous and it was seized upon with glee by the founders. It is a fuzzy and comforting assumption and hugely important in creating a greater public awareness of the reality of alcoholism as disease—that very progressive neurological disease.

What's new is that the genetic predisposition has been mapped. Silkworth was right and the founders of AA knew it!

The alcoholic liver functions abnormally from the git-go. When alcohol hits this abnormal liver, it is broken down, first into acetaldehyde, a.k.a. ethanal. This is not a good guy. It is the first and most lethal of the metabolites produced in the breakdown of alcohol. It is a carcinogen and leads to cirrhosis and many forms of cancer. It is also present in tobacco smoke, car exhaust, and embalming fluid! This is the most important and most toxic ingredient in this lethal metabolic stew; the feces in the punch bowl. It has even been suggested that alcoholism should be renamed "acetaldehydism."

In alcoholics, the acetaldehyde builds up to a degree 50 percent greater than in nonalcoholics. The liver works hard to break it down further into a nontoxic acid but the excess acetaldehyde hitches a ride out of Dodge on any of a number of substances, including red blood cells. Soon enough this toxic gatecrasher finds its way to the brain. Think of Keith Richards circa 1971 at a church picnic to get a sense of the deep nastiness involved.

When these rock and rollers come to town, they go into a mating frenzy, capturing the neurotransmitters for a quickie between neurons and receptors. The offspring is a whole new crowd of chemicals: the tetrahydroisoquinolines (TIQs). The TIQs are party animals. They like to feel good, and the host of the dance, the brain, likes to have them around. They are the backstage drug dealers at any decent concert. Small wonder. The TIQs have nearly the same chemical structure as opiates, the sleep-inducing, pain-relieving drugs. Lullaby and good night.

The brain then begins to crave more TIQs. Sound familiar?

So here is the final cause, the primal mutated thirst behind alcoholism.

Not quite. Research has found another glitch in the system. Enter DNA. In 1990, researchers found a mutation in chromosome 11. Called the A1 allele, this mutant is present in the DNA of 70 percent of individuals who have died of alcoholism. This science is still new and there are sufficient fuzzy areas that no bold statements have been made. But the research continues.

Meanwhile, back at the rock and roll concert in the brain, we find an anomaly that is particularly interesting and fruitful. Researchers found that in individuals with the A1 allele mutation, there were 30 percent less available receptors for dopamine. Less receptors, more craving. The brain gets high on the very first hit of alcohol and wants that high again and again. So far, so good. The brain, however, stimulated by TIQs, starts producing more and more opioid and dopamine receptors. So in order to feed the craving, greater and greater numbers of TIQs need to be fed to the craving brain. The capacity of the now drunken brain increases. The slaking of the thirst is a full-time job. All that was noble and good is sacrificed to the thirst. Alcohol has subverted the hierarchy of needs to the most reptilian urges. Spirit is sacrificed to a voracious serpent, deep in the most ancient parts of the brain where the only needs are reactive. With any stimulus, any stimuli at all, there are only four reactions. Fight it. Flee it. Feed on it. Fuck it.

Genetic abnormalities and receptor deficiencies describe the disease. I buy that entirely. But does science make the "alcoholic personality" a myth? I don't think so, and all the science in the world does not exempt the alcoholic from the responsibility for his actions. We will look at that reality, just ahead, as the brain is washed clean of its sewage.

Several weeks after this conversation, Stephen and I had lunch with, happily, no particular agenda at all. Over cheeseburgers and iced coffee, we wandered happily in each other's minds. Irony and paradox are never far away when we talk. In the context of a larger conversation, Stephen reminded me that alcoholism is a neurological disease with a spiritual solution.

Indeed.

Here was the first glimmer that my personal odyssey was going to lead to unknown places as I moved from cause to effect, to change, to effect of change. Karma.

But there's more.

CHAPTER SIX

Shrink to Fit

I've been est-ed, rolfed, processed, NLPed, Jungianed, Gestalted, and Alexander-ed. I've sat in the presence of an oracle in the Himalayas who was costumed in gold and silk as he twirled and swung his swords and uttered guttural predictions. I've been trans-personaled, de-personalized, insighted, and reframed. I've been painfully probed for energy obstructions and introduced to my inner child. Or my inner brat, more often. I've floated in isolation tanks and consulted the *I Ching,* astrologers, the tarot deck, and sand drawings.

I'm a child of my middle-class upbringing, in awe of the power of the many faces and masks of psychology, that most garrulous of social sciences. Freud, Jung, Adler, Rogers, Janow, James, Hillman, May, and Von Franz share shelf space in my mind with Shantideva, Krishnamurti, and Meher Baba.

In all of this turning and searching I made only one fundamental mistake: I thought that I needed to be fixed.

I would like to think that it was not Carl Rogers I needed but Fred Rogers, telling me, "I love you just the way you are."

I wasn't ready for Mr. Rogers yet.

Such was my unknotted conditioning that I was drawn to them all. I will always be grateful to the greatest of those teachers, with the gifted and empathetic Norma Simon, Ph.D., of New York City, at the top of the list. I do not regret a moment spent in these endeavors. I also believe that any therapies that I undertook during my days of active drug addiction were largely wasted. Such treatment was of a creature, me, so defended and deluded that only minimal insight was possible. I was the masked man. In my best moments, I still saw my problems as having external causes. Alcoholism was a foe to be defeated. Mr. Hyde so thoroughly repressed Dr. Jekyll that only the shattering insight, yet ahead, into my principal coping strategy of drug addiction, would break the chains. Jekyll needed the gift of desperation.

In those years of therapy undertaken while addicted, I recall only one moment that was to inform me of my future. I was seeing a Jungian therapist in San Francisco. We dealt, predictably, with dreams and those errant associations I made with them. I think my doctor was perhaps frustrated. Time and again, he would bring up the possibility of alcoholism. Time and again, I would assure him that I fully intended to take steps to deal with it. Time and again, I got drunk on the nights I meant to go to AA meetings. On one of the days that would be one of the last of our encounters, after I had settled into a soft leather chair and we had exchanged assurances that we were each just fine, thank you, he handed me a sheaf of photocopied letters. This would be a gateway to the interior that I would see only from the distance of many years.

His office was a comforting place with totems, crystals, and water-carved rocks on shelves. There was a brilliantly colored Huichol yarn drawing of the Mother of Peyote above his desk. I had studied, haphazardly, the shamanic path of the Huichol, an ancient civilization in the Sonora Desert, and had such a painting myself. Leathers and dark woods predominated the room. I had been nasty drunk the night before and I had the shakes. My skin didn't fit and my head hurt. I appreciated the warmth and rich aesthetics of this place.

The letters he handed me were the total correspondence of Carl Jung and Bill Wilson, some of which is quoted in chapter 5. That was my first exposure to these letters and I did not understand them at all. Inside of me, Hyde snarled.

The doctor's impulse was a good one and it has taken me twenty-five years to grasp those teachings.

Such are the coincidental moments that stick.

The inquiry remained as the years of drunkenness dimmed in a receding past. Was there some psychological reason for my condition? I was an only child for twelve years and when my brother was born I happily took on the role of caretaker. When our parents went out at night, I fed him and then rocked him to sleep, singing one of the only two songs I knew the words to, at twelve: "The Ballad of Davy Crockett" and "The Tennessee Waltz."

Was I taught the caretaker role? No! Why pathologize brotherly love?

My father was, by his own admission, an alcoholic and my mother was clearly a classic codependent. That term has had a hard time of it in the recovery community, being stretched to wrap up a number of woes. When I first learned it, it meant only one thing: the alcoholic is wrapped around the bottle; the codependent is wrapped around the alcoholic. It is the bottle that runs them both. That is all. I had lived all over the map by the time I was seven years old. I was sent away to the family farm on most summers and sent to various summer camps, against my will, on other occasions. I witnessed fights between my parents. Parents fight, lovers fight, friends fight; we're only human. But I didn't know that then and seeing the gods fight was frightening.

Both of my parents' families were chockablock with alcoholics, including a total of three alcoholic uncles. Dad quit drinking, or so it seemed, when I was nine and became what might now be called a "workaholic." I don't see it that way, however. He put the energy of his alcoholic days into rebuilding his shattered academic career and then parlayed that energy into a rich creative life, authoring several books and gaining increasing respect for his work. His work would finally lead to his being considered the "Father of the Middle School."

I outlined the conditioning I learned in this family in chapter 2. I don't believe that my conditioning was any worse or any better than most other folks'. But a distinction begs to be made. Not all conditioning is negative. It's useful to be free of it all, but I have found it important to do so as the "fair witness," without ratings and comparison. I was conditioned to see war as an answer to aggression. I was conditioned to see women as subservient to men. I was conditioned to believe that medication was the first line of defense against pain. I was conditioned to defend the helpless and disenfranchised. I was conditioned, clearly, to question authority. Much of this conditioning happened both within my family and outside of it.

When I rebelled, in the early 1960s, that rebellion was violent and hurtful. When, by 1967, I had dropped out of the social structure almost entirely, I caused more pain. I do believe that my conditioning, together with an unconsciously compliant nature, led to those rebellions.

I do not think that my conditioning had anything to do with my addiction. My addictive brain kicked in when I had that first hit of alcohol and went into hyperdrive when I added amphetamines and downers to the mix.

I can see now that my Jungian analyst in San Francisco did not consider alcoholism to be the cause of my dysfunction. I believe he saw that the alcoholism needed to be confronted before any other work could begin. Addiction built a wall around me, keeping out pain and love and fear. Addiction built a wall within me, to the same purpose.

If my childhood had been the same, without the family taint of alcohol, my rebellion and dysfunction would most likely still have happened.

Addiction made it easier. Drugs became the solace for my grievances until the day that all that remained was the grief of late-stage alcoholism.

After more than ten years of sobriety, I spent three years in therapy. The unconscious was made conscious. I could see the conditioning that had unmade my life and began to work on it. Yet, nowhere in that good hard work did I find a cause and effect for my addiction. I only found its allies.

I believe that the God-seeking thirst is one useful explanation. I believe that the religious use of drugs is an explanation. I believe that therapy can point to the coefficients of addiction but not to its causes. I believe that scientism is an explanation. If I had to champion one cause, it would be that of addiction as being located in a mutated brain.

I have dwelt in all those houses, with beneficial results and with results that were not so beneficial. But the question remains. Is there one cause for my addiction? No, I reckoned.

Then what question am I missing? What is it that I didn't see?

I went back to the poem by Bhartrihari. After listing his searches, his dead ends, and his folly he says of himself:

. . . but never shed craving—
never obtained a single pierced
cowrie shell.

My thinking was diseased. In my drunken years I sought the way *out,* not *in.* Such were my thoughts as I continued the search for cause. During my sober years I have continued, intermittently, to seek an explanation when, I now see, such seeking is itself "craving." The cause of my latest disease was the intense desire to understand my suffering. That is a good and useful answer but I am unable to put aside this desire. I am neither stoic nor enlightened. My spirit remains restless and unsatisfied. Beneath every answer was another question.

I thought I chose not to feel all the wonder of aliveness, and that addiction just happened to be built in, to aid me in my folly. It was that thought itself that was the greatest folly of all. Sitting with it and assuming without examination that it was true, I continued to take all the wrong paths. If I had not taken those wrong paths and dismissed them, I might never have found the path I could finally walk in equanimity. In reality, there was no wonder of aliveness in me, except as a distant ancestral memory. There never had been such aliveness, except on the rarest of occasions. Drunk or sober, child or adult, I was estranged from my most vital environment: the very world into which I was born. So are the vast majority of us in the civilized world.

There are lots of paths to the gates of hell and an equal number for the return journey. None of the ones outlined in the previous chapters spoke to me with any authenticity. The scientific hypothesis *assumed* causality. The psychological one was narrow, excluding the larger world of which we are all a part. The mythopoetic, the hero's journey, seems to be a dangerous conceit for me, with the assumption that alcoholism is, again in the words of Dr. Jung, *"the equivalent, on a low level, of the spiritual thirst of our being for wholeness."* Perhaps, but that is a dangerous assumption for someone as prone to inflation as I am. Dr. Jung himself cautions us not to get stuck in the metaphor.

The shamanic journey is probably the closest metaphor to what I now believe to be true. It is earth-based and has an atavistic consciousness that is compelling to me. But my use of psychedelics, like the majority of my confreres, was just to get blasted and weird. It was only after I stopped that I could find the authentic shamans.

Each of these etiologies was useful, but limited and limiting. I looked at them as an aggregate, but found nothing new. I had added up the parts, but I didn't have the sum. I knew that there was some quality that bound these ideas together, but I didn't know what it was.

It took a bottle-nosed dolphin and a poisonous snake to bring me to the base metaphor. It then took meditative practice to make that metaphor real in my life.

In the fall of 2004, I made what I quickly saw would be the first of many trips to the Osa Peninsula of Costa Rica. With the publication of this book, in fact, this peninsula has become my other home. The Osa is still a primitive spot. The infrastructure is wretched, with potholed roads and trails that are overgrown within weeks of being bushwhacked. There are few of the precious entertainments of the civilized world. The principal— indeed the only—town, Puerto Jiménez, has a population of less than 2,000. The town feels like a final frontier, a town from the Old West. In fact, until the establishment of the Corcovado National Park in 1975, this little town was a center of gold mining and logging. That spirit still remains. I also saw a few gringos there who had a familiar demeanor to them; folks who perhaps had been involved in a type of commerce that finally made disappearing into the jungle, and staying permanently south of the border, the path of wisdom.

On this first trip I stayed at a lodge on the Osa Peninsula that was right on the beach and that backed up to the beginnings of the Corcovado wilderness.

It seemed to be the Garden of Eden, even to a man accustomed to the natural beauty and wildness of northern Florida. Eden, the place of dwelling for the innocent ones, before the Fall. This Eden is as well the fecund home of wild nature that defies our concretized and romantic ideas of the Biblical Eden or the Pure Land of the Buddhists. Make no mistake; the Osa

Peninsula is a funky place and is not hospitable to the seekers of the "primitive luxury" so often offered at $1,000 a day in some of the more remote and idyllic island paradises.

The day I arrived, I barely made it to my little house before the rains came. I had only heard of monsoons or seen representations of them. I don't know that this rainstorm was truly a monsoon at all, but it was at least the closest to one that I have ever experienced. The rain seemed to come straight down, in gouts rather than drops. My little home had a thatched roof and a deep porch, half of it roofed and half open to the sky. I sat on the covered porch for a half an hour or so, blissed out and grinning like a kid who had snuck into a blues bar, and then, prompted perhaps by some ancient code, I stripped off my clothes, stepped out on the unprotected deck, and stood in this enormous vertical river.

Behind me lay the darkness of two troubling years and, more recently, the results of a national election with implications that frightened me. Standing in the rain, I felt cleansed. I laughed aloud and thanked the gods for their mercy.

Over the next few days, I explored the rain forest and the jungles. I ate well and slept well. I had brought along a book on physics, of all things, which I quickly abandoned, and read, instead, the first two volumes of *His Dark Materials,* a trilogy of great power by Philip Pullman.

I walked the mile-long beach, often the only person treading those sands. I was at peace.

I met a young couple from San Francisco and shared most of the meals with them. We talked of this and that: travel, their joyous wedding during the brief time in SF when same-sex couples could enjoy that ceremony, my despair over the recent election, and, no doubt, cabbages and kings. Three days before they were to leave they said they wanted to go looking for wild dolphins and asked me to come along. Sure. Cynical by nature and a Florida resident as well, I was fearful that this would be a manu-factured trek, free of adventure, risk, and uncertainty. You know—Mouse World. We hired a boat that afternoon and would head out in the early morning.

The couple was afraid they would be disappointed. That the cost of the boat and captain would be wasted. I told them, with no idea what I meant, that I would try to conjure up a dolphin for us the next day. We ate a late supper and headed off to sleep before our early wake-up the next morning.

Back on my deck, I remembered my promise. Dressed in sarong and cigar I stood on the forward edge of the deck and let my meditation-trained mind drift out over the darkened Golfo Dulce. I asked to contact a dolphin. I visualized some seeking part of myself moving across the waters. Soon I sensed a great animal and a connection with it. I continued to stand there. I went more deeply into the state of single-pointed attention and then even that was gone. This was contrary to everything I had ever believed was possible. I had been quite a critic, gently so, of the "new age" hustle that was taking over some parts of the re-covery community. It seemed to me that quite a few folks in early recovery are eager to have an out-of-body experience before they ever have an in-body one. I still think that.

But this night, something happened.

I don't think I stood there for very long, but when I "woke

up," I had dropped the cigar and my body was moving in the strange and undulating rhythm of an infant in deep water.

I was nonplussed but the magic of the Osa was boiling in my heart so I didn't bother to figure it out.

The next morning, not twenty minutes from the dock, the captain shouted and pointed to a fin approaching us rapidly from near the shore. It was a large bottle-nosed dolphin. Flipper, for heaven's sake!

I was stretched out on the foredeck of the small boat and the dolphin swam directly at the boat, at the deck, at me. The captain slowed us down and the dolphin stopped at the bow, stood up out of the water, and looked straight at me. He seemed to hang there for a long time, Michael Jordan taking a jump shot, and then flipped backward into the water and came up again, quickly, on the starboard side. He looked at me and then submerged and swam alongside the boat for a while.

On his back were strange markings that reminded me of nothing more than Chinese calligraphy; one bold stroke and other smaller ones fading to the sides, like the limbs of a phantom tree.

Without thinking, I rolled off of the bow and into the water with this . . . this . . . this shaman! He kept his distance but slowed to my pace, as I lay on my back and paddled with sweeping motions of my arms.

It was over quickly, this visit to a larger world. The dolphin swam off, I climbed back into the boat, and we continued on. Later, we found a large pod of spinner dolphins and swam with them, towed behind the boat and surrounded by these sinuous mammals. Later yet, we crossed to the other side of the gulf and had a lunch of huge sandwiches, with tomatoes and avocado and sharp cheese on hunks of dark bread. I recall with some silly joy the moment when one of the women had the courage to say what all three of us were feeling.

"I need to pee."

I jumped off on one side of the boat and the women on the other. Men's Room, Women's Room.

That night I stood on the deck again, sans cigar. I skipped the trance this time and just allowed myself to feel again what I had felt that day.

Connection.

I had crossed yet another bridge, a wild one to wild places that now seemed as familiar as my own limiting skin once had. The walls around my "knowing" were cracked a bit wider open and would soon tumble entirely. Days passed and my body/mind got softer and less defended. The warmth of the place welcomed me.

Only days before I was to leave, I went for a hike with a small group of new friends. This hike was through private land in the Corcovado, the home of our guide Alfredo. Within an hour it was clear that this was no mere hike. Alfredo had bushwhacked the trail several months earlier and it was visible only to him, it seemed. We passed through densely canopied primary growth forest and waded creeks that had slowed to trickles. We gained and lost over a thousand feet of altitude, no mean feat in those lowlands. Blessedly, all of us on the trip had sufficient reverence for this great cathedral that we kept our mouths shut and our minds open.

What we had thought would be a two-hour hike became, at its end, a four-hour one. Two hours into the walk, we stopped for water and to rest awhile. The undergrowth was too dense for sitting, so we stood in sunlight, surrounded by grasses and trees of a bewildering variety. I stood a few feet from a strangler fig, one of the most bizarre trees in that or any wilderness. These twisted giants are members of the fig family. In Costa Rica they are called *mata palo* or "killer tree." In the elegant phrases of my friend Juan Carlos, "Monkeys eat figs and then go shit in the top of a tall tree. The fig seed sends roots down inside the other tree and then to the ground and then they grow up, eating the host tree. The host tree suffocates and leaves this hollow tree behind."

I stood near this cannibal, greedily drinking my tepid water. A woman standing near me and to the side, with a clear view of the strangler fig, said, "I wonder what kind of snake that is?" and pointed at one of the myriad pockets formed by intersecting roots. I looked straight at the snake, coiled just at my eye level, three feet away, thinking I could help her out with my vast knowledge of serpents, gained in my south Florida childhood.

I knew this guy, for certain.

"It's a fer-de-lance," I said, "and it's a good idea to back away."

I didn't move an inch.

The fer-de-lance is the most dangerous snake in Central America and kills more people annually than any other American reptile. When this guy strikes, his hypodermic fangs inject an average of 105 mg of venom. The fatal dose for a human is 50 mg. It's a pit viper and a close relative to his jungle companion, the bushmaster.

I felt a rush of chilling exhilaration in the presence of this creature from a world I did not then know. I was in the presence of "other." I was transfixed, hypnotized, suicidal, some would say, standing close to Mr. D. himself, in his diamond-patterned suit. There was a sense of powerlessness here far greater than that I felt when I ran into a bull shark years before while diving in the Virgin Islands. I think, perhaps, that when I met the shark I was not as awake to my own mortality as I was on this hot rain forest afternoon. Everyone else moved back. I stood there.

My spell was finally broken as the rest of the group began to move on, closing water bottles and grumbling. I joined them, unhappy that I had forgotten to bring my ubiquitous black notebook.

We were all grateful and deliciously tired when we finally got back to our truck for the bone-jarring trip back to the lodge, anticipating a cold shower followed by a searing hot bath and rest.

Then we found out that Alfredo had lost his machete somewhere in the jungle and needed to go back to find it. It didn't take long, happily, but we would have backtracked the entire trail to find it if necessary.

Such is the balance between this wild place and the humble men and women who live in it. The jungle is appreciated and it is respected. In this untamed part of Costa Rica, machetes are ubiquitous and the jungle forbidding. It is a fair balance, tilted toward the jungle.

On the bumpy return trip, my friend Lauren and I opted out of the final fifteen minutes of the overland ride and walked the beach route back home, a calming and invigorating forty-five minutes along persistent high surf and hot, hot sand, with a sun so intense as to send any wise creature scuttling for shade.

Wild jungle, wild saltwater. The sun and the salt and the recent memory of the resting pit viper began to pry old ideas loose and a new one began to grow. What if it is our estrangement from wild places, from the ancient rhythms of growing, withering, dying, and blossoming again that are at cause for the plague of addictions in the "civilized" world? Why had I felt so radically sober in the presence of the serpent?

It is worth mentioning that at the final rest stop, back in the jungle, thirty minutes after the encounter with the snake, I felt, for the first time in twenty years, a desire to drink. The taste and rush of ice-cold Stolichnaya in a crystal tumbler, right there in the jungle, collapsed my wild mind into mere thirst. It lasted only a moment and I quickly and easily dismissed it. Unlike the biblical serpent, this fer-de-lance offered a total and terrifying freedom, a reentry into the world I, we, left behind many generations ago, or a quick exit from this one into the eternal. The quick desire for the icy alcohol was a fear response, I believe, to my lifelong fear of the very real.

My mind wandered as I walked the beach in silence with my friend. Perhaps it was the wide expanse of sand, the silence, the recent experience with the fer-de-lance and my own inchoate musings that brought up the next totally unexpected image, but whatever the alchemy, I am grateful.

In 1968, I played the narrator in a reader's theater adaptation of Saint-Exupéry's *The Little Prince*. There were only three actors and we worked on a nearly bare stage with only a large box, which served as a hiding place for the actor who played every part in this presentation but the narrator and the prince. She wore a black cocktail dress and pearls. The prince and the narrator were in white tie and tails.

I suspect that if you are familiar with *The Little Prince,* you know exactly where I am going with this.

Right. The snake.

In the story, when the prince plops to earth in the Sahara Desert—in exile from his home planet, and wandering the cosmos in search of a way to protect his beloved Rose—the first being he encounters is a snake, "a coil of gold, the color of moonlight," which "flashed across the sand." The snake is wise and playful and confident. He speaks only in riddles because, he claims, he can solve all riddles. He is the bringer of death. In a story about mysteries, the snake is the only absolute. He is Kali, "the Black One," who in Hindu cosmology is the bringer of death and *the destroyer of ignorance.* It is the snake who offers the way home.

I had encountered a snake—*the* snake—and the jungle was buzzing with life and expansiveness. My ignorance, the illusion of separation, had been further chipped away. I had crossed another bridge, this one to the wider natural world and the rhythms of life and death.

In the Prayer of St. Francis of Assisi, often associated with the practice of prayer and meditation in Alcoholics Anonymous, we are told, "It is by self-forgetting that one finds. It is by forgiving that one is forgiven. It is by dying that one awakens to the Eternal Life." In those three simple phrases I find selflessness, atonement, and awakening. As I pray that prayer now, each morning before seated meditation, I feel compelled to shorten the final stanza to "it is by dying that one awakens."

Face to face with the fer-de-lance, I had slipped into a state of no-self. In Zen parlance, body and mind fell away. The separate egoistic self had yielded to a power greater than itself and had heard the whisper of the divine in the slight wind in this primeval place.

The snake in Genesis brought the fall from grace. The original sin. This snake taught me that I was always falling, in a state of original grace. I was not expelled from the Garden, but welcomed back to it.

That night, after a long soak in a hot Japanese bath under the stars and supper with my friends, I sat on my deck and mused. What were the teachings of the dolphin and the fer-de-lance? The dolphin had been gentle, inviting me to a greater sense of aliveness. The snake had been fearsome, inviting me to die. What they had in common is that they lived, ecstatically, in the world of sensing and spontaneity, in the eternal presence of life and the immanence of death.

They were fully alive. I, in spite of years of training in Asian philosophy and practice, was still somnambulant. Sometime, somewhere, somehow I had been severed from my primal roots. Why else would I have felt such a sense of homecoming and ecstasy? In my estrangement from the larger world, I had suffered.

I wondered if this primal wound might have something to do with my alcoholism, with my constellation of addictions.

I think so.

In Homeric times, the dolphin was seen as the merciful side of a vast and dangerous ocean. Other cultures, such as the Māori of New Zealand, consider dolphins to be the messengers of the gods, guides to safe passage through difficult straits. Aristotle said, "The Dolphin is not afraid of a human being as something strange to it, but comes to meet vessels at sea and sports and gambols round them even when under full sail." In northern Australia there is a belief that dolphins became humans in dreamtime.

The snake has had a harder time of it, particularly in the Bible. But consider Quetzalcoatl, the plumed serpent, the master of life, not death. Australian aborigines associate a particular giant serpent with the creation of life itself.

Aesculapius is said to have discovered medicine when he saw one snake using herbs to bring another snake back to life. Hence the modern medical symbol of two snakes wrapped around a staff, the "caduceus." Death and life, co-arising, as they always do. The medicine and the illness treat each other, arising together.

"My" snake and "my" dolphin were messengers and creatures of mercy. Just ahead of me was a deeper appreciation of the roots of my alcoholism and a greater release from that bondage. My teachers were that scarred dolphin and that lethal snake. I am grateful.

It would take months of meditation and inquiry and reading but I finally saw that isolation and anesthesia were not the result of addiction, but its cause. The escalating plague of addiction in the "modern world" in so-called first world countries was the result of a flight from and destruction of the natural world, which longs for our return.

The picture is a dark one. There are no heroes here, no

monks, no gentle therapists, and no patient researchers in bright laboratories. There is a foul darkness at the center that threatens to engulf us. The few remaining indigenous tribes are falling into addiction to alcohol, drugs, and nicotine; the aborigines in Australia suffer from an incidence of addiction to drugs, alcohol, and nicotine that reaches as high as 80 percent of the population. A friend who is a Native American tells me that in winter, members of his nation are often stacked along roadsides, like cordwood, dead from exposure after sniffing gasoline. These are those very Native Americans who, long ago, were pronounced to have a "genetic predisposition" to alcoholism. I don't think so. The arrogance of such a presumption is deeply troubling.

I think that these cultures share with all of us a genetic predisposition to an intimate connection to the earth. The genetic predisposition to alcoholism and addiction of all kinds is, I believe, a mutation, born of estrangement and fear. The aborigines, the Native Americans, all the poor and disenfranchised can become our greatest teachers—if we learn to listen.

I did not need to be fixed. I wasn't "wrong"; everything else was out of balance, off the mark. In this life of off-the-mark lies my deeper "sin." I did not need to look to narrow ideas. It was this entire system that was diseased.

What I had thought of as "my" pain was "the" pain. The pain of separation is not unique to me. Treating only "my" pain misses the mark. This unbidden primal wound does not absolve me of responsibility. To the contrary, it makes taking responsibility all the more urgent. The original breaking of the illusion in Jim Morton's office was only the beginning. It was there I realized my connection with my fellows. Now the snake and the porpoise were showing me a larger ignorance and a larger kinship.

I needed to realize that the self is me in the world. If it was the power of estrangement that caused me to live a poisoned life, I believe that there is an equal power of reconnecting that can heal the entire system—me in the world.

For any alcoholic, the first awakening is the acceptance of the reality of one's own alcoholism. That one adamantine moment can set in motion an ongoing enlightenment. It's a choice, of course. But once chosen, the awakening, the enlightenment never ends. It was this random encounter with the primal world that opened my heart to the reality of unfolding enlightenment, a knowledge that until then had been only a matter of conversation.

In the Golfo Dulce and in the rain forest, I moved from the head to the heart, from a world of knowing to a world of feeling.

Each awakening is a beginning, not an ending. As I had seen some months before, this is a crucial understanding. To miss it is to sink into delusion once more and, as I had found, to live a suicidal life, in the grip of Thanatos and his fawning charm.

As each answer appears, it brings another question. In the distance are more bridges to cross.

CHAPTER SEVEN

Bringing It All Back Home

When my son, Will, was twelve years old he began the life of a New England preppy, heading off to the Fay School in Southborough, Massachusetts. All of his aunts and his uncle on his mom's side had gone to boarding school as had all of his cousins on that side of the family. It wasn't an easy decision and there are still days when I question the wisdom of it. He was enthusiastic to give it a try and, at this writing, he is thriving in that atmosphere.

The day he left, I gave him a small paperback copy of the *Tao Te Ching*, telling him that someday he might want to read it. I assured him that there was no pressure to read it. Less than two months later, Will called and told me that he was a Taoist! I shrugged this off until he then began telling me why, even mentioning specific verses of the book. His favorite was verse eight, part of which (in my version) serves as the epigraph for this book.

I was happy that he had found such wisdom and comfort in this ancient book and I believe that it is telling that a child of the twenty-first century would be drawn to a book so rich in earthy metaphors and so uncontaminated by self-consciousness.

During my high school years, I developed affection, largely

self-serving and dilettantish, for Zen Buddhism and Taoism, particularly the Taoism of the *Tao Te Ching*, the same book I gave Will decades later. I was drawn to that confounding book written over 2,500 years ago by a former Chinese civil servant named Lao Tzu. Unlike Will, I did not understand it at all. Perhaps an understanding of that text was not as urgent to me as it was to Will. Nonetheless, to this day, my understanding of that ancient book is meager, but my affection for it goes far deeper than in those days of eager exploration, decades ago.

What I have found in this book today and my suspicions of why Will and many of his peers are drawn to it is crucial to an understanding of the deepest roots of our addictions and to their cessation.

For centuries, scholars have disputed whether or not there ever was such a man as Lao Tzu. Some have suggested that the *Tao Te Ching* was compiled over a matter of centuries, added to and subtracted from to serve the military, social, or political ends of succeeding dynasties. Perhaps. More troubling has been the position taken by some scholars that this book was one of military strategy, or of political theory, or, perhaps, just a collection of sayings. They dismiss Lao Tzu's imagery as primitivism or metaphor. Such are some scholars. That misses the point. They are applying the rigid assumptions of the modern age to a work that predates such assumptions by many centuries. Like some science, some scholarship is distancing.

Recent scholarship, by the poet and translator Red Pine and the Chinese scholar Tu Er-Wei, points to an understanding of Lao Tzu and the *Tao Te Ching* that is not stuck in these modern categories. I find a resonance with their conclusions as I sense them, far beneath mere intellect. What follows is my take on their scholarship, filtered through my own experience, and cooked in my particular skillet, and for which only I am responsible.

Lao Tzu was alive during what has come to be called the "Axial Age" (800 to 200 BCE), as were Confucius, Gautama Buddha, Zoroaster, Plato and Aristotle, Jeremiah, Ezekiel, and Isaiah. This was a period of great unrest in the Mediterranean basin; all was "awry." The times were changing and our ancestors, arguably self-aware for the first time, were in the midst of war and economic expansion and the falling away of the smaller city-states.

This should sound familiar. According to Catholic theologian Ewert Cousins, drawing on the work of Pierre Teilhard de Chardin, there is every indication that we are in a second Axial period. There are signs as well that we are seeing the death throes of the monotheistic religions and a necessary evolution toward a universal spirituality.

Primal consciousness, that consciousness before the Axial period, was tribal and often shamanistic. These "primitive" tribal cultures lived in intimate harmony with the turning of the seasons and the cycles of fertility and barrenness. They lived, mythically, with the greater cosmic cycles. They were a part of nature and celebrated its harmonies with ritual and myth. The tribal consciousness was vital to the life of each member of the tribe. The tribe, in a sense, was one organism, intimately related with the larger natural world. Separation from the tribe meant death, spiritually or physically, and other tribes were seen as threatening and hostile.

The consciousness that emerged from the Axial period was an

individual, "self" consciousness. This consciousness was reflective and analytical, giving birth to science, philosophy, and new religious institutions that served as structures for self-reflective spiritual paths. The Greeks said, "Know thyself." The Buddha said, "Be a light unto yourself," his final utterance. All the individual-oriented great religions of our times were born during the Axial period: Judaism, Taoism, Confucianism, Hinduism, and Buddhism arose from this soil, and Judaism laid the groundwork for the arising, centuries later, of Islam and Christianity. Each of these, to different degrees, taught individual enlightenment, individual moral responsibility, and individual identity, separate from tribe and separate from nature. In some traditions, there were radical schisms between self and nature, matter and spirit, heaven and earth. God and man. Consciousness had become subjective. The Self was born, yearning for Heaven and separated from the Earth. Empiricism trumped experience.

It was into this environment that Lao Tzu was born, in the Huhsien Prefect of the state of Ch'u. The place of his birth, in that epoch, is the difference that makes a difference. Unlike the other states in that fertile region of China, Ch'u remained a shamanistic culture, although to what degree it is impossible to know. Lao Tzu was immersed, therefore, in a culture that encountered the sacred from an earth-based and mystical consciousness. His Taoism, his only book, the *Tao Te Ching,* was deeply indebted to this primal and ecstatic earth consciousness. These cultures were deeply immersed in the fertility cycles of the natural world and to the larger cosmos of which it was a part. They felt themselves, as well, to be part of a tribe, made whole and sacred with ritual and myth.

I believe, without the certainty of empirical evidence, that it was this subtext of a spiritual connection to the earth and to the cosmos that so entranced my son, a child of the brave new world of "this and that, getting and having," with science and empiricism venerated, and the monotheistic religions of the world corrupted and in decline.

Such consciousness has not been wiped from the face of the earth; our deepest programming is still for the Paleolithic. The primal consciousness is still with us—with Will, with me, with you—but it is hidden, surfacing only in dream and myth and art and in the rare gift of being able to be surprised.

At the heart of the spiritual life is the ability to be amazed. Open horizons suggest it to us. Deep meditation is a journey into that consciousness, for those able to take it. In Will's case, he found it in print, that great achievement of the Axial Age. For me, it took a snake (see chapter 6).

The estrangement continues to accelerate and more and more of us are slipping into addiction, seeking the ecstasy (consider that word in its current drug implications) and the connection that continues to fade. Our foods, our waterways, our land, and our own bodies are laced with toxic chemicals, some of them, dioxin for example, a product of anthropogenesis.

The first response to trauma is disassociation. For an animal in the wild, that is a useful coping strategy, cutting off the pain of the circumstances in order to be alert and defensive. The ongoing techno-madness of our culture is only a predictable outgrowth of the deterioration of the promise of the Axial period. We are traumatized by our separation from the earth and we disassociate, most vividly in virtual reality. Virtual reality is controllable at the push of a key or the flick of a switch. The Epcot Center, a jarring advertisement for the future, controlled by those who wish to control the future, offers gentle education into the world of virtual reality.

The wound of estrangement produces solutions that only deepen the wound. When I drank myself to a fare-thee-well, the only cure for my illness was to drink more. I was living a poisoned life, chemically created and chemically treated, that had me astride a grave.

This is old news. Members of my generation were calling attention to these horrors, both social (in their corporate costumes) and ecological, many years ago. In fact, the ecological situation has improved. London, for example, is habitable and healthy where not too many decades before it had been foul with soot; the air was toxic. It would be foolish indeed to claim that ecological degradation is new. It is not. Consider Easter Island, for example, which was for unknown millennia a tropical paradise and then in the space of only a handful of centuries after it was colonized became a mysterious wasteland.

Like addiction, however, what begins slowly accelerates to the point of disaster, unnoticed. The perceived cure becomes deadly and disassociation continues.

We are on the cusp of personal and ecological disaster. In the techno-madness of the first world, the entire culture is behaving addictively. We consume more and more and get less and less satisfaction. There is no probative difference between substance addiction and the constant and escalating desire for status, wealth, prominence, or, the most banal of all, fame. There is no probative difference between the individual denial of substance abuse and the social denial of the destruction of the earth. Both are a movement toward death and both are fed by endless appetites and obdurate denial and, in the felicitous phrase of Zen Master Thich Nhat Hanh, they "inter-are." Former Vice President Al Gore said, "I believe that our civilization is, in effect, addicted to the consumption of the earth itself." And here is Thich Nhat Hanh again, in a commentary on a story told by the Buddha to his monks: "We are eating our country, we are eating our earth, we are eating our children."

This is a dark picture. The estrangement escalates. Addiction escalates.

And yet, people are seeing the edges of the darkness and are turning back toward the light. Addiction recovery escalates. There is a worldwide tribe that says "We" not "I." I stopped drinking and using drugs in 1984. I did it because I wanted to. I was able to do it because there were other people just like me who wanted me to as fiercely and resolutely as I did. As a tantalizing aside, it is instructive to see that membership in Alcoholics Anonymous in the United States has been static for over a decade. In Asia, it is increasing dramatically.

In the late spring of 2005, I was at a gathering of sober people who were supporting each other in the desire to remain sober. The conversation was boring, frankly, as one person after another recited the usual nostrums and slogans, without much juice or freshness. After some time, a woman who is new in the sober world said something that got my attention. I listened closely. I was hearing a new voice of recovery, although I suspect she was unaware of it. I was, at the time. What follows is a fictionalized version of that statement, but it is true to its meaning.

"I've lost my sense of place. I just got back today from the outer banks of North Carolina and I don't recognize it any longer. My family has lived there for generations and it is the place I have always considered to be home. Since the hurricanes of years back, laws have been passed and traditions violated and now the place I loved is overrun with condos and fast-food joints and the beach is so littered that you can't walk on it without shoes. When I was younger, that was where we had bonfires and made love in the dunes and sometimes sat and talked all night and now it's gone. It's awful. It's not something I'll drink over, I don't think, but I'm hurting. Like I said, I've lost my sense of place."

This is not a typical statement at gatherings of this type and the majority of the people in the room were nonplussed. "So what? What's your problem?" There were giggles and some of the oldsters arched their eyebrows and smiled, condescendingly. I was one of them. But the statement grabbed me and wouldn't let go.

She had told the deepest truth, however unconsciously. She was threatened, not by change, as the land developers might claim, but by a further wrenching from the soil and environment from which she was born. She hadn't linked this violence to the land to her own violence toward herself, but there was a deeper knowing that something was terribly, terribly wrong. In his brilliant and challenging book, *Wild Hunger*, Bruce Wilshire says, "on some level of consciousness, many of us still feel the will-of-the-place, our alienation from it." ("Will-of-the place" is the etymological root of *wilderness*.) I believe that to be so and I believe that it continues to insist on being heard, more loudly and persistently than ever. The time has come to listen. In the depths of my addiction, I most wanted to be free. I was hopeless and peace entered. It's time to listen again.

The healing of the primal wound was necessary if I was to be fully alive, in the present moment, useful to my family, my fellows, and my home. I needed to be "radically sober." *But how?* I wondered. I recall that Thich Nhat Hanh says that we must build again the bridges we have burned.

I dreamt outlaw dreams in that 1967 summer in the Haight-Ashbury, when I was long-haired, skinny, flat-eyed, and high on cheap wine, acid, and speed. All freedom was gone as I lived an illusion of freedom, trapped in fears and nightmares. I wore the outlaw costume and kept busy with the whirl of music and sounds and sex and movement, always movement away from the present to the next, the next, and the next. Just over there was what I wanted and the Outlaw Boy would find it. I was the outlaw who faced his fears, I proudly boasted, but with no true sense of what I was truly afraid of. What were those things I feared and could not acknowledge?

Just this: Self-knowledge. Simple stillness. Simple silence. Solitude. The road to the interior was too grim and too frightful. But this radical desire, this outlaw urge, was there; it was just stuck to an idea of the outlaw that was corrupt and useless. No different from Jesse James. I had to stop using drugs and drinking to get some sense of what it represented for me.

I live outlaw dreams today, in my sixty-third year, while in my house in north Florida. I wake up before dawn, just as I did as a boy in my far-off Tennessee childhood. I brush my teeth. I take the prescribed aspirin to forestall another TIA. I make coffee and sit on my back porch, weather permitting, and drink it. I light a candle and some incense. I sit cross-legged on a black cushion on a larger black cushion on the floor. I take a breath as if it were my dying one. I exhale. Inhale and exhale, the original breath I breathed, you breathed, on and on until it ends. I sit for an hour, sometimes longer. I work. I tend to the bonsai tree that Will gave me for Christmas a few years back. I might go to a local bar and dance to zydeco rhythms. I pray, daily. I cook, I clean the kitchen. I feed my cat. How perfectly ordinary!

What of those outlaw dreams? They weren't, in hindsight, very different from Jung's idea of the corrupted spiritual journey. (I'd best be careful of inflation with this one.)

I see them now as an acknowledgment of, and movement toward, a deeper consciousness, a *radical sobriety,* a part of bringing the unconscious to the conscious and acting in a way more deeply resonant with the innate human capacity for love and kindness and happiness. It is to consciously live the life of *bodhicitta,* the mind of enlightenment. Radical sobriety is not about not drinking, but it has no reality in the life of any alcoholic when that life includes drinking. It is to live outside of the demands of the many, the marketplace, the worldwide corporate impulse toward the material and the scientific. It is, more important, to live outside of these demands without hating them. The angry outlaw is no outlaw at all, but an unwitting supporter of that which he opposes with such public energy. To be radically sober is to answer the human longing for peace through developing inner peace. The only law is the law of Karma, the reality of cause and effect, beyond our understanding but endlessly responsive to our actions, right here, right now, in only this present moment. The small self is relinquished and the prayer of the emerging greater self is an endless offering of gratitude through action. This alone is the liturgy of the present moment; thank you, thank you, thank you.

To be an outlaw is to be radically human. It is not about looking disdainfully upon a culture we are not a part of; that is vanity and solipsism. It is not about a "create your day" mentality, which is just the old self-centeredness wrapped in the clothes of the new age emperors. There are as many outlaws on the Pennsylvania Station New Jersey Transit 5:17 commuter train to Dover, New Jersey, as there are in the distant hills of the Siskiyou Mountain Range.

To sober up is a radical act. It is to confront the shadow rather than simply name it. German philosopher Nicholas of Cusa said "In God all opposites convene." To come out of the dark to find the light that exposes awareness but does not blind, and to be open to finding God, spirit, the mind of the Buddha, the Tao, Brahma, is an act of courage, compassion, and will. It is a radical act.

The T'ang emperor once asked the Taoist sage Ssu-Ma Ch'eng Chen (who was responsible for introducing "inward gazing" or what we would call insight meditation, to Taoist practice during the T'ang Dynasty), "How can I cultivate the Tao?" Ch'eng Chen answered, "Minimize your desire, embrace simplicity, and practice non-interference."

As the earth is healed, I am healed. As I see the sacred nature of this ordinary world, I begin to sense the sacred in myself. When, in any small way, I can notice the arising and falling away of the natural world, I am learning the rhythms of my own brief life. T'ao Ch'ien knew that this one round, this "hundred year life," was all there was, that there is no life but this actual one and he resolved to live it in the very heart of its turnings.

After years free of chemical dependency, the prophecy of 1 Corinthians chapter 12 finally came to meet me: "For now we see in a mirror dimly, but then face to face; now I know in part but then I will know fully, just as I have also been fully known." Attuned at last to the greater song, and dancing the greater dance, I had come to life. T'ao Ch'ien was headed toward Hogtown Creek.

Atonement and unfolding enlightenment were becoming one thing. As I have tried to live by the words of Ssu-Ma Ch'eng Chen, with faith in the words of Paul, I entered the realm of simple-hearted contentment.

SIMPLE-HEARTED CONTENTMENT

Here, once more, is the poem by T'ao Ch'ien.

People praise Yen's benevolence, say
Jung mastered the Way. So often empty,

one died young. Always hungry, the other
lived to a ripe old age. Their names

outlived death, but they eked out such
haggard lives. And renown means nothing

once we're dead and gone. Simple-hearted
contentment—it's all that matters.

We coddle thousand-gold selves, but
we're only guests; change soon takes

our treasure. Why not naked burial?
People need to get beyond old ideas.

T'AO CH'IEN

CHAPTER EIGHT

Breakthrough

October in Atlanta, Georgia, is a time of perfect weather; there is a gentle atmosphere around this most cosmopolitan of Southern cities in the late fall. That's how it seemed to me, in any case, when I left the nastiness of the coming winter in New Jersey in 2000. I went to Atlanta to escape more than just weather. My divorce was in process and I was raw and on the run.

I went to Atlanta to visit friends and to enjoy the remaining traces of the Old South that still cling to this place. The chain bookstore there was friendly, unlike the cold indifference of the one where I shopped in New Jersey. The coffee franchise had comfortable tables in the warm sun. I think the coffee was better, too.

The ostensible reason for my visit was to attend a conference at Emory University on the teaching and legacy of Zen Master Dogen (1200–1253), founder of the Soto Zen School. The Soto school is based in diligent effort to awaken and emphasizes seated meditation *(zazen)*. Dogen taught that there is not a "moment's gap" between the aspiration to awaken, practice, enlightenment itself, and dwelling in the reality no-separation (nirvana). Kazuaki Tanahashi says of this idea of Dogen's, "In other words, there is no authentic practice that lacks enlightenment," and then goes on to say, "*unfolded enlightenment* is initially sub-conscious awakening, which is spontaneously merged with conscious awakening at the moment of breakthrough."

For example, when we addicts first see the reality of our addiction (that is, that there is no separation between ourselves and the illness), we are seeing, at a level beyond understanding, the world as it is. At that initial moment of breakthrough, we see something we always knew, without knowing we knew it. Think about it. Wasn't there always a sense that something was terribly awry and that there was a way to get back on the tracks? The wheels had come off and you knew it. The cry of "Is this all there is?" would never arise unless we had faith, already, that there was an answer. Enlightenment itself unfolds, but we only see that when breakthrough occurs.

In the life of the addict, the authentic knowing that the illness and the cure arise together is to fully grasp that unfolding, for the first time. Aha! *I AM* an alcoholic. There is no separation. Alcoholism is not something out there; it's right here, right now. This, again, is atonement, at-one-ment, with illness and cure. The so-called "surrender" of the First Step of Alcoholics Anonymous (see appendix 1) is not a surrender at all; it is a seeing-through the veil of separation to the reality of a "new understanding of mind, self, human relationship and power" in the words of anthropologist Gregory Bateson. This initial breakthrough is of remarkable power as it is nothing less than an entire shift in the way we think.

We're in a hopeless situation and that's a good thing because to hope is to have some vain wish that thus and so will happen if we just do the exactly perfect thing. What we have is not hope, but faith. We wouldn't ask the question without knowing there was an answer; that's faith. What we see through is far more valuable that what we go through. The path has always been right beneath our feet and, at the moment of awakening, we see it!

That initial enlightenment is to see the path.

Imagine it this way. You are in a place of complete and utter darkness. There is no landscape, no comforting feel of rails or steps, and no sense of where the land might suddenly end at a deadly drop-off. Nothing moves; there are no breezes to indicate tunnels through rock faces if, indeed, there are rock faces at all. You might be on a bridge or on an endless plain. You are lost, entirely and utterly, without hope. This is a hopeless situation, but there is faith that there must be some unknown way out.

You are still. All at once, there is a radiant stroke of lightning and your landscape is revealed. You can see tree lines and peaks of distant mountains and, beneath your feet, the outlines of a path leading straight ahead to that—to what? That house? That shelter? That emerald city?

Awakening is that flash of light in the darkness, en-light-enment, which makes you aware of what has been there all along. To awaken is to shed light on awareness.

This highly simplified excursion into the complex world of Dogen-Zenji is important to living on the path of unfolding enlightenment.

At the time of the conference in Atlanta I was a student in the Soto lineage. My teacher was going to be there and I hadn't seen her in over a year. We arranged to meet for a moment before the conference began. It was a touching moment for us both, as she had been my staunchest friend during the early days of my divorce. It was in those difficult days that she sent to me, by regular mail, a handwritten note with the words that I have endeavored to keep in my consciousness ever since, and have paraphrased throughout this book. I think this is the most important teaching I have had thus far.

She wrote to me, *"We cannot possibly understand the millions of vectors of cause and effect which are impinging on our current situation. We can only use what happens to us in service to our primary purpose of awakening and freedom."*

There is no blame, no analysis, no theology or psychology in those words. They are a simple statement of the truth. I believe that whatever happens could not be any other way. I believe as well that it is not what happens but what you do with what happens that makes all the difference. By the end of the Atlanta conference, her great wisdom would come back to me with an even greater power than when I first read it, in her precise handwriting, on good paper.

I attended this conference in the hopes of immersing myself more deeply in the teachings of Dogen. That was not to be. Instead I formed a strong friendship with a Zen monk from North Carolina, a tea master and all-around good guy. I deepened friendships with people in Atlanta and came to appreciate that city more. I had a respite from the sad happenings in New Jersey and was able to seek the shelter of wisdom, teachers, and community.

There was another, greater benefit of this trip when I heard the one statement I needed most to hear.

These conferences can be deadly to anyone who is as impatient and squirmy as I am. During a lecture, just as in meditation, it is remarkably easy to drift into fantasy or internal conversation while giving every appearance of being attentive. (Teachers can tell when you've gone away; that is one of the great values of that relationship.) The speaker on this drowsy afternoon was Taigen Dan Leighton, a Zen priest and the author of several books on Zen practice. Toward the end of his talk, almost hidden away in his impressive scholarship and formidable presentation, he said something that brought me out of what was probably an erotic fantasy, the most common type for us lazy meditators. It was this paraphrase of a great poet and longtime Zen practitioner and pioneer: *"Gary Snyder says that Zen comes down to meditation and sweeping the temple and it is up to you to decide where the boundaries of the temple are."*

Such a remarkable idea, this, and applicable across the entire spiritual spectrum. Presbyterians, Sufis, Hasidic Jews, Catholics, Twelve Steppers, heathens, and Buddhist practitioners can all practice daily worship consonant with whatever form is home to them. I meditate daily. You may do matins and vigils or simply ask God for guidance during the day. What I see in this statement by Gary Snyder is the true simplicity of the spiritual life and that it is exactly the reality of this intense simplicity that requires full and thoughtful attention to the present moment. When praying, pray. When meditating, meditate. When sweeping the temple, sweep the temple. It is so human to slip away during such times as in my behavior during the conference in Atlanta or, often, the attention that I pay to my prayers, such as they are. You, too, I imagine.

How often have any of us been in church and joined in with the prayers, the hymns, the chants, the doxology (that most

Buddhist of the Christian liturgy!) without any sense of what we are doing? Simply paying attention to this worship or practice will deepen the sense of the sacred arising from our distracted minds. Ten minutes of prayer or two hours of meditation are each to one purpose: to connect. To connect to God, to self, to Atman, to the immanent other, or to the breathing of the earth, the cosmos, the entire phenomenal universe itself. The starting place for this connection is exactly where we are and is based entirely in our experience to date. Therefore this spiritual practice, however soft, however fixed, must be constantly renewed or it is only yesterday's news. We must be always beginning.

Part of my daily ritual is a vow to save all sentient beings. I'd better mean it! If I say that and am, at the same time, adjusting my shirt or recrossing my legs to a more comfortable position, then it is clear that the only sentient being I am interested in at that moment is me and my own comfort. Our prayers, our chants, our creative muttering in an attitude of meekness and self-forgetting must be attended to with a full *shin,* that potent Japanese word implying heart and mind working as one, with an absence of emotional judgments based on desire or aversion. "I want, I want, I want" does not fit on the cushion or in the pew. When I do walking meditation by Hogtown Creek, I may look with gratitude at the flowers just beginning to bloom or I may notice with dismay the rusty beer can washed downstream by yesterday's torrent of summer rain. That's a start. That same walk, taken in nonjudgmental awareness, is mindful walking. At-one-ment, that is.

On an intensive meditation retreat I attended, the teacher

asked us to go out into the redwood forest that our center was comfortably nestled in and find a tree to sit by. At night.

I found my tree, set up my cushions, and began to watch my breath, the ultimate connector to all life, sentient and insentient. As usual, I drifted at first. I considered what a wonderful notion this was; this practice of connecting to the ancient redwood grove and I began planning the telling of the story of it. This one spun out for a while before I caught it and returned to my breath. Then here was a crack—a loud crack—of breaking deadfall, trod upon by what was most likely Sasquatch himself in this Northwestern forest. I wanted a cigarette, and I don't smoke.

Return to the breath. Romance and terror were able to find their wormy ways into my meditative mind with great ease and only moments apart. They did not come from somewhere else. I created the romance and I created the terror. (Sasquatch helped with the terror part.)

This business of dwelling in the present moment, or praying mindfully, is not so easy. It is astonishing when you realize that it is fully one-half of what Gary Snyder says is spiritual practice. Over the years I have seen concrete evidence that the meditative life is constantly unfolding and deepening. Early on, I was able to see my early conditioning clearly, but it was only after years of practice that the subtleties of that conditioning began to surface. What a joy! This business of meditation has no end.

What about the other half of the poet's statement? What is it to determine the boundaries of the temple and keep it clean?

It is here that my teacher's words began to find their way to places in me that were still raw. She had turned over rocks covering my own appalling denial. I found that merely to see my conditioning and to become at one with it and then to move on and make amends for its effects were only a beginning. There was a greater task ahead.

I was "fine." I had done the Steps of Alcoholics Anonymous, years before, and had internalized the ones about daily self-examination, meditation, and prayer. (See appendix 1.) This was not entirely so. It is daunting to realize what a spacious reservoir of conditioning and unfinished business I can find, if I look, or if, more often, someone points me toward them as my teacher did on that day.

Finding the boundaries of the temple and the ongoing teachings of the mundane events and openings of my daily life are interrelated. As my awareness broadens, so do the boundaries of the temple. In my early days in AA I had learned that my sobriety was contingent on the daily maintenance of my spiritual condition. In my larger spiritual life, I had seen that this unfolding enlightenment was itself contingent on ongoing practice, new every day.

Ever so slowly, I began to learn to dance, to cook, to walk, to stand still, to touch the earth, all practices among myriad others that are the North Star upon which my compass is always fixed. I recovered the connection with the earth that had been severed millennia ago, and only decades ago, in my days of being on it.

I had finally seen that it is not a selfish and inward-gazing wholeness that I had sought, so loaded is that idea with the potential of just more self-involvement; nor was it recovery from alcoholism; nor was it God I was looking for. I sought, as Jim Morton had taught me, years before, *connection*; with hearth,

earth, and heart. I also had learned that I would not find them by looking, thinking, or investigating. Back in that Central American rain forest, I had moved from the world of thinking to the world of feeling. In Alcoholics Anonymous there is a marvelous promise that "We will intuitively know how to handle situations which used to baffle us." This intuitive knowing is precisely that feeling way of essential being that I had found, at last, to be my preferred and my principal connection to the world with which I had always been connected without ever sensing it.

Now it was personal.

(a personal connection w. health, earth, + heart

CHAPTER NINE

Coming to Life

My friend Papa John, who brought the words of Paul to me during my meltdown, has also given me the gift of touching the earth. In early summertime, John gives away the abundant crops of his garden. His gift to me has been pints of plum tomatoes and a beautiful and fragrant basil plant. I make Papa John's tomato sauce with them. Here's what you will need to make a tomato sauce of your own:

1. Papa John or someone similar who grows their own tomatoes and basil. It's important that this person understand what Papa John does and that he remind you of it when he brings you some tomatoes and a basil plant. Here is Papa John's understanding: A man is never so tall as when he is on his knees in the garden.
2. The tomatoes and the basil plant, of course.
3. Salt and freshly ground black pepper.
4. Olive oil.
5. An open mind, dwelling in the present moment, relaxed and aware.

First, wash the tomatoes. Take your time. The water beads beautifully on the brilliant skins.

Then, chop the basil, which you have snipped from the plant just moments before. Notice the fragrance. You should use a very sharp knife for chopping the basil, one of those Chinese ones if you have one, which give you the opportunity to pay very close attention to what you are doing. Bunch the basil up and then chop it with a rocking motion, the tip of the knife continually resting on the cutting board as you push the basil, a bit at a time, under the moving knife. Pay attention!

Now, quarter the tomatoes. Use the same knife and don't wash it beforehand. Quarter the tomatoes carefully, one at a time. From time to time, pick up a piece and smell it. Savor the moment. Take some time with this. This is slow food, not fast.

Put the chopped basil and the tomatoes in a heavy pan. I use an old cast-iron skillet that holds the memories of many fine meals. Turn the heat to medium high and cover the pan. Listen. Sniff. You will hear the tomatoes as they begin to render their juices. You will know from the smell that they are beginning to break down. Check them from time to time as you don't want the pan to get dry or the tomatoes to scorch. It should take about ten minutes for the tomatoes to break down completely. Notice how the scent of the tomatoes begins to change as they cook. What might you call those differing scents? Green? Woody? Piercing? And what about the scent of the basil? What happens when those scents begin to blend? You'll know when the tomatoes are ready, I promise you.

Put the cooked tomatoes through a food mill. Put a bowl

under the food mill and begin to press the tomatoes down with a tapered wooden pestle. Notice how easily the tomatoes are reduced. When you use a food mill like this, you don't need to peel and seed the tomatoes first—the mill does it. Food mills have been around for a really long time and are a joy to use. Toward the end of the pressing process, you can run the pestle around the inside of the food mill, wipe it off into the mill and do it again.

The sauce is almost ready. Take a moment to consider what has happened. Botany, chemistry, and physics have been involved already.

Who cares! Put the sauce back in the pan. If you wish for it to be a bit thicker, cook it at very low heat until it's just as you want it.

Add the salt, pepper, and olive oil. How much? A smidgen, a pinch, and a drizzle ought to do it. Taste the sauce and smidge, pinch, and drizzle some more if you think it needs it.

Now. What to do with it? Do you give the sauce to your own special Papa John, in gratitude for his gift? That's a nice idea, but I'm not sure that it honors his great generosity. Generosity in Sanskrit is *dana* and it has a flavor of sacrifice and of giving to an equal. With *dana* there is no ego involved, only a desire to express love. So far, then, you still have your sauce.

What else could you do with it? You could cook up some pasta, grill a piece of red snapper, and serve the pasta, sauce, and snapper with a touch of peach salsa. That would be a nice thing. But you should tell Papa John about it, don't you think?

I think that an important thing to do with the sauce is to

remember how you made it, write the recipe down if you wish, and then tell the tomato sauce story when you want to remember your connection to your friends, your hearth, and the earth.

Papa John says that getting on our knees in the garden is a good thing. Indeed. We settle into the humus when we do that—the earthy soil of our origins. *Humus* and *humble* have the same Latin root and imply low watery places as well as low estate or being. It is in this darkest of ground that growth begins, humbly.

Making Papa John's tomato sauce is all the alchemy I need: this simple alchemy of spirit and matter.

This is the only way that we can heal, this sacred alchemy creating a theology of the earth/self. We must come home to the wholeness of all of life, not to a limiting and self-serving wholeness of the illusory individual psyche. That's yesterday's news. We must make holy that entire community of the sacred trinity of earth, hearth, and heart. We cannot focus on one—they already are one. This vital reconnection is not about politics or economics or even religion. It is about expanding the sense of self, the reality of the boundaries of the temple, until nothing is "outside."

My wounds are not "my" wounds, they are "the" wound, the wound of separation. I am responsible for that healing, just as I am responsible for that wound. The "terrorists" are not out there somewhere. The terror is created right where each ordinary person stands, in ignorance of the wounding of the world. When I burn lights I don't need, or fail to say "no" to my own desires to be entertained, endlessly, by some corporate entity or to the political candidates who would exploit the earth and the poor of the earth, then I am responsible for the ongoing war against the earth. The list of "sins," the ongoing illusion of separation, is endless.

The first Axial period, covered sketchily in chapter 7, was a turning from tribal consciousness and connection to the earth, to self-consciousness and an ongoing disconnection from the earth, with the gods elevated to a place far above, a heavenly place of air and spirit. The earth was left behind and disdained. People began to worship politics and economic growth at the cost of the earth. The earth was wounded and we were wounded, in heart and hearth. The scourge of addiction escalates, and we all lay wounded. *Scourge* is from the Latin for "whip." How apt. We have learned to whip ourselves with addictions until the addictions become the whips which drive us.

Now it is time to see that we are in the second Axial period, another time of turning, of the transformation of consciousness to a global and ecological spirituality. If we make it.

It is in this practice of mindful cooking and many other mindful activities, that we can begin the process of reconnection with the earth. We see the sacred in the ordinary, with mindfulness.

A large part of the spiritual awakening promised in Twelve Step programs is an awakening to what we always knew: that we are alive, alive on a living earth. It is clear that much of that knowledge is ancestral, nearly obliterated by the progress of finding large solutions to small problems. Today we need small solutions to large problems. There is no political agenda here. The Taoist poets and saints lived apart, reducing desires, embracing simplicity, and practicing noninterference. Their example endures. They didn't, as commonly assumed, "do nothing." Not at all. They did nothing other than live exemplary lives and when the larger structure made demands of them that were contrary to their way, they refused. This refusal to cooperate begins at home, in your temple, and mine.

Let's relinquish our whips and slow down. My actions *are* the difference that makes a difference. Your actions *are* the difference that makes a difference.

When I get up each morning, the first thing I see is a magnificent piece of calligraphy of the word *tai,* which in the context where I found it (the *I Ching*) means *peace.* Each morning I am reminded of peace. Each day I endeavor to be peace.

There's a simple and familiar road to that peace.

If we are addicted, as Al Gore said, to the consumption of the earth itself, then perhaps the way out of the world of addiction and into the world of freedom is to admit to that addiction and our powerlessness over it. Once the denial of the addiction is broken, and we are able to see what horrid damage we have done to this earth and to see further, that it is our estrangement from this earth that made addicts of us in the first place, then, hopeless, we break through to seeing the troublemaker.

I am addicted to consuming the earth—my life has become unmanageable. For readers for whom those phrases are not familiar, they are a paraphrase of the Twelve Steps of Alcoholics Anonymous. (See appendix 1.) For those in Twelve Step programs who might be concerned about traditions being broken here, let me assure you that I don't think AA should have any involvement in anything other than helping others to recover from alcoholism. If a concern persists about this public use of the Steps for a problem not related to alcoholism specifically, let me offer this, from AA cofounder Bill Wilson: "Though the essays which follow [in the book *Twelve Steps and Twelve Traditions*] were written mainly for members, it is thought by many of AA's friends that these pieces might arouse interest and find application outside AA itself. Many people, non-alcoholics, report that as a result of the practice of AA's Twelve Steps, they have been able to meet other difficulties in life. They think that the Twelve Steps can mean more than sobriety for problem drinkers. They see in them a way to happy and effective living for many, alcoholic or not."

Breaking through to life as it is and then studying deeply those personal qualities that have kept one in the prison of isolation and fear are not new. Nor is it a new idea to confess those sins and to atone for them. Such a way of life far predates Alcoholics Anonymous and, in fact, even the Christian principles upon which it was quite rightly founded.

We're all addicted to something, if addiction is the assumption that there is something, somewhere outside of ourselves, that, when we get enough of it, will make us okay even though the getting of it causes just more thirst, more hate, more ignorance, and more suffering. As it always will. Our escalating thirst for money, sex, and power enthrall us and the greater social structure is more than happy to feed those endless thirsts. I bought a Harley Davidson motorcycle not long ago, and before it even got to the dealer, I went back and added a high-performance package to it, to make it better, and even then, with delivery only days away, I decided I had gotten the wrong model and nearly went back to cancel the order for the Sportster and replace it with a Springer Soft Tail like my friend Mark's. I didn't.

I also woke up, finally, and realized that a Harley for a man of my age and reckless disposition was a foolish choice. This was during the meltdown and in retrospect I saw exactly what I was up to. There are lots of ways to kill oneself, you see. It is also true that there are very few material objects in which money, sex, and power are all present and to such a vivid degree! I sold the motorcycle the day I got it. I never even went to the dealer and looked at it.

No thing is enough. The addiction for power creates the need for power and love dies. The addiction to sex creates the need for more sex and love dies. The addiction to money only creates suffering, finally, and on a global level love dies. And the earth weeps. This multitude of addictions, some subtle, some grotesque, keep us on the course of certain destruction until that moment when we can say, "I'm the problem. I am the cause of all this suffering. I, alone. This addiction is in me, not elsewhere."

Then and only then, at a point of helplessness over the way we are consuming the earth, can we begin to put an end to it.

My friend Bock says that if he were asked to rewrite the Twelve Steps, he would make only one substantive change. He says that Steps Two through Nine would each have a sub-Step. That is: Step Two will be followed by Two "b," Step Three by Three "b," all the way through Step Nine. The "b" Steps will merely say, "See Step Eleven." Step Eleven is the one that counsels prayer and meditation in order to find God's will and the power—the love, I would say—to carry it out. I agree. If we are willing to look mindfully at our past behaviors, step by step, and the remarkable damage they have done, to us, to our children, to the earth, and to our own hearts, we will be free, happy, and joyous. To paraphrase another AA phrase: I do not think that is an extravagant promise.

Here we are doing what must be done. We are searching out the root causes of our addiction(s) and atoning for them. It's easier for alcoholics, of course. We are driven by desperation and if the greatest danger is in our continuing estrangement from the earth, then you can bet that we will set that straight. If, as Bill Wilson has stated, the future of AA is in "emotional sobriety," then the reunion with our true selves is that very emotional sobriety. We are on our way home only after we look at what our behaviors have really been and see how we have caused harm. We begin to see through our heedless consuming of the earth and robotic denial of the harm of our endless attraction to the baubles tossed our way by the consumer culture, political and economic, and the entertainment megaplex. When you are eating, simply eat, and notice the food before you. Where did it come from? How many people were involved in getting it to you? I would suggest that if you don't know the answer to either of these questions that they are very important ones for you. My daughter is a cook, a cooking teacher, and an organic farmer. Here is her philosophy, in her words, telling about her business, Kam's Kookery.

> Our philosophy at Kam's Kookery is twofold—to celebrate the joy of eating and living well. . . . We also seek to support sustainable agriculture. Humane and sustainable agriculture produces safe, wholesome food in a manner that is ecologically sound.

Eating with the rhythms of the earth is eating with emotional and, I'll add, spiritual sobriety.

Look at the food on your plate. How has it come to you?

I gave up television some time ago. I still have a set and I watch DVD movies on it and it is often on when Will is here. I have so much more time now without television and so much more energy. My mind feels clean and sharp. One of the precepts of the way of the Buddha is "Do not cloud the mind." In the Buddha's day this statement referred to the use of alcoholic beverages. Over time it has changed to include narcotics and other drugs. I believe it has an even deeper significance. My mind is clouded by noise and by flickering images on a television set. My mind is clouded by the barrage of advertisements and by the sad urgency of the newscasters, who are not providing the news at all, but only fear. I don't miss television at all. By freeing myself of the toxins of television, I am healing the earth. I am not constantly being told to buy, buy, buy, fear, fear, fear. In healing myself, I heal the earth.

I have learned the practice of looking deeply. I do not practice it well, but I do practice it, and over time the practice has strengthened. I have only given a few examples in this chapter. I hope you will find a practice of your own. The world depends on your practice.

Here is the task I set myself, years ago, that still is the tether of my ongoing journey to earth. There is one question I can always ask myself when I am considering any action, or following any train of thought: *Where is the joy in this? Am I protecting joy or am I causing suffering by this action or this thought?*

I went on a trek in the Himalayan kingdom of Bhutan in April and May of 1999. This was my second trip to this enchanted place. We flew into Paro, Bhutan, from Bangkok, stopping in Calcutta on the way to pick up additional passengers. The flight from Calcutta to Paro is considered one of the most beautiful in the world. For the last hour or more, the plane is in, not above, the Himalayas. This is VFR (visual flight reference) flying only. If the weather is such that you can't see the mountains, you don't go. When you can see the mountains, they are close by. Farmers on the steppes, cultivating chilies and rice and winter wheat, are clearly visible. Everest skulks in the distance, black and ominous.

The day was clear and when we landed at Paro, there was time to chat and wander while our duffels were going through customs. I was talking with a friend's daughter and enjoying the fresh mountain air. When she turned her back to me and bent to pick up her duffel, her T-shirt rode up and I saw a bit of a tattoo spreading on her lower back. I asked her about it, so she pulled the shirt up to show it to me and to a few others who were standing nearby. It is a magnificent tattoo. It covers much of her lower back. Her own design, it is largely Celtic, with soft edges and circles in shades of pastel.

Three years previous I had gotten a tattoo on my upper left arm. It is the Tibetan script for *Om Mani Peme Hung,* a chant associated with Avalokiteshvara, which loosely translated means, "Oh the Jewel in the Lotus Aum." For Tibetans it speaks of a longing for liberation for the sake of all sentient beings. I had always wanted a tattoo but never found one I liked until I met the film producer/writer and adventurer Masha Nordbye in Bhutan on an earlier trek. She had had this script tattooed on her arm in Lhasa. That was it! That was what I wanted and I got it done soon after my return.

On this afternoon, three years later, Jessie's dad, Sam, wandered over, wondering, I'm sure, why his daughter was lifting her T-shirt and one of his best friends was taking off his shirt and showing off his upper arm. When he saw my tattoo he said what I had said to Masha three years before, that he had always wanted a tattoo but could never find the one he wanted. This wasn't it either, but we decided that one aspiration for this trip would be to see if we could find one he liked. He was finally ready, at age sixty-eight, to take the plunge. I had waited until I was fifty-five. (Good thing; otherwise, I might have spent my life with Tweety Bird or some other grotesquerie on my shoulder as a very young friend of mine has done.)

Two days later, we were visiting the Planned Parenthood office in the Bhutanese capital of Thimphu. I was feeling a little off so was waiting outside while the rest of the group listened to a presentation by the resident directors on their efforts to encourage the Bhutanese, particularly the young people, to practice birth control.

Sam came bursting out of the offices, practically running, holding a cloth carryall bag in his right hand, waving at me. "This is it. Here's my tattoo." On the bag were colorful representations of two Tibetan icons. One, a circle with three congruent swirls of blue, green, and yellow was contained within the other, a traditional square. The circle was the icon for joy and the outer square, the icon for protector. Taken together the symbol indicated protector of joy.

I looked more closely at the bag. The design was certainly beautiful. But . . .

"Sam, this is an advertisement for condoms."

"I know, isn't that wonderful? The protector of joy. I'm going to get it!"

I got the tattoo as well, a month or so later when Sam was in New York on a promotional tour for a book he had written about the trapeze. We went together to my tattoo artist, deep in the East Village. We had worked on the design throughout the trek, pestering our fellow trekkers for their ideas. There was now a little swirl of "joy" escaping the protection, with a replication of the larger icon, still within the protective borders. We can't overlook that the protection was the message; joy has to find its own level, unfettered, and risks must be taken and lessons learned.

So I wear a bowdlerized condom advertisement permanently etched on my right arm. I take that charge seriously: to protect joy.

Mindfully considering our actions and our thoughts, we can ask deeply, "Am I offering joy or am I offering suffering?" Another way to ask the question is, "Am I living in the world of exploitation or the world of nurturance?"

As I have continued, fitfully, living the life of radical sobriety, I have experienced firsthand the reality of the teachings of Gary Snyder, in my home, on the earth, and in my heart. The boundaries of the temple began to expand on their own. All that I had to do was follow.

CHAPTER TEN

A Will to Love

As in 1 Corinthians, the "face-to-face" teachings had begun in earnest. I had received this face-to-face teaching with wonderful teachers: a snake, a priest, a scholar, a dolphin, a Vietnamese monk, and a pediatrician in Oregon. They all gave me the parts. It took finally recognizing one more teacher to show me the sum. I had looked more closely at how my consuming habits were affecting my home, my family, and the whole of life. I am deeply imperfect. It is the very imperfection that reminds me, again and again, of my vows and my humanity. My teachers had done well.

The great teachers let you see your path without telling you where it is. They simply walk their own path, without looking from side to side, straight ahead with constancy and faith. I believe, as well, that in every life there is one true teacher, that one who touches us in new and tender places. That one true teacher has as many faces, as we can see.

When I met my true teacher, in 1989, I began, haltingly and with many diversions run by my self-will, to finally detect small glimpses of my enlightenment, unfolding. As the unfolding continued so did my connection to this teacher until the day that I finally recognized him, years later.

My father was known as the Father of the Middle School. In 1964, he envisioned—in what my brother, Phil, has described as Dad's "road to Damascus experience"—the possibility of a radical change in the way that primary and secondary schools could be structured. The middle school, which Dad championed, is now the prevalent model of secondary education in this country.

One day after he had retired, I was sitting in his office in the house that is mine now. The office was filled with books, as it is now, and there were plaques on the wall honoring his accomplishments. It was a summer day and Dad and I were relaxing, talking about not much at all. I noticed a new plaque, which, as all of them do, honored him as the Father of the Middle School. I said to him that he must feel happy to be remembered that way, to have given such a gift to the culture.

He looked at me for a moment, saddened by introspection. Then he said, "I would rather be remembered as the father of my two sons."

That is his legacy. That was his deepest teaching to me. Born of remorse, and staggering insight and humility, it was what I would recall most vividly years later when I was given a chance to be father once more, having failed so entirely the first time around.

I remember my father as my father, the man who, just on time, opened his heart to me and invited me to accept his love.

In a commentary on the first line of verse eight of the *Tao Te Ching* (which appears in my version as the epigraph of this book, and which is most elsewhere translated as, "The best are like water") the scholar Li Hung Fu said, "the best alone choose humility . . . What they choose is what everyone else hates. Who is going to compete with them?"

So, to be the best parent requires humility. In my drinking days I knew nothing of humility. This affliction continued for many years into my life free from drugs and alcohol and persists to this moment. Humility is more often misunderstood than grasped. It is not about embarrassment or humiliation. In fact, a life of true humility makes embarrassment or humiliation impossible. Living humbly, we are unlikely to compare or compete ⨎ and it is comparison and competition, giving rise to self-centered fear, that creates a life of persistent dissatisfaction and longing. "I'm not enough." "I'm not like him, he's better." "I need more so I can be like my neighbors."

It was in my father's connection to me, indeed, in the connection of any parent and child, revealed in love and nurturance rather than fear and power, that I could begin to overcome the family affliction of alcoholism.

Dad's grandson, my son Will, was born at 8:45 p.m. on November 15, 1989, in Beth Israel Hospital in New York City. The labor was brief but the delivery was difficult. His mother, Pauline, and I agree to this day that those final minutes of his birth were the most achingly intimate in all of our years together. We were in a birthing room, softly lit and quiet. This was natural childbirth, with no drugs save joy and hope. However far she and I may drift from each other, we have a bond that no one can put asunder.

Face to face, our eyes only inches apart as I knelt beside her, we breathed together; we conspired to bring this unnamed child into this world. Face to face, her pain hurt in my belly. Face to face, she felt my anxiety as I glanced at the fetal heart monitor and saw the child's pulse slowing to a dangerously low level. The doctor, Robin Phillips, was fiercely compassionate although Pauline remarked later that sarcasm at a time like that is not forgotten. Robin said, "Okay, we can no longer wait for the perfect moment."

Moments later Robin threatened to use forceps to get this child out of the danger, fearful that the umbilical cord might be wrapped around that fragile, tiny neck. Pauline got angry with Robin, I saw, and in that deeply controlled determination often born of anger, she pushed, harder and harder, her face streaked with tears of pain. I forgot myself. There was only this woman, who I loved beyond mere love, stricken with pain and desire. There was only this incomprehensible process of life coming to the light, terrified and naked. There was only this mother, this father, this child, as one life.

It was eight minutes from that point of the final hard push until the child entered this great cosmos, alone for the first time, severed forever from the great physical intimacy of his mother's body.

As this miracle, gender still unknown and nameless, first began to emerge into the light, Robin said, "Oh my God, look at the size of this baby." Pauline was not thrilled but I was, not too secretly, thrilled. It's one of the vanities of fatherhood to think that you alone are somehow responsible for the full and robust masculinity of a boychild. We don't just check to see if there is a penis, but to see how big it is! Such vanity.

At birth our child weighed ten pounds and four ounces.

Pauline is a small woman. So concentrated were Robin and the nurse on getting him fully and safely born, that it was left to me to check and then announce, "It's a boy." I don't know if I screamed it or whispered it, but everyone heard it. I think Robin and the nurse were embarrassed. That's not the daddy's job, after all, it's theirs.

During the pregnancy we had chosen boy names and girl names. The two for a boy were Lucius (Luke) and William (Willie). I saw that this was Willie, without a doubt. A few minutes later, his mother said the same, not knowing my thoughts.

He looked like he had gone twelve rounds in the Olympic Babyweight Boxing finals and had won, but not without suffering some mighty hits. He was bruised and red, streaked with blood and amniotic fluid, and filled with the primal rage of a wolf in a steel trap. This was a place of metal and light and noise. Behind him lay a matrix of potential, composed of safety and warmth and love. I believe it is that very matrix, writ large, that we long for on this earth. The small miracle occurs for those who see that the earth itself is that very matrix.

The nurse placed Willie on the warming bed and cleaned him of the gore. He tried to turn over, from back to belly, a first for Robin. She was astonished still, first by the struggle, then the unanticipated size, then his stubborn attempts to do things his own, instinctual, way.

I picked him up, surprised at how I knew exactly how to hold him, carried him to his exhausted mother, and put him on her breast. Her hands rose and she held him. The eternal Madonna, incarnate once more. She embraced Willie gently, the ancient maternal drive in full blossom. I don't think I had ever seen such pure love and I doubt I have seen it since. Willie told me, years later, "I think I love Mom more than I love you. I've known her longer."

Amen.

Thus was my teacher born.

He was ten pounds, four ounces then. As of this writing he's fifteen years old; six feet, four inches tall; 165 pounds of kick-ass rock/blues guitar playing, Chinese-speaking, Taoist-aspirant preppy; described in his school newspaper as "the talented fresh-man" musician, playing guitar and mandolin and bass and ukulele; a gentleman with shaggy dark hair and hazel eyes.

Like all of us, he's been through a lot in fifteen years. All of his grandparents who were living when he was born have died. He has seen his parents divorce. He has, after difficult delibera-tion and discussion and the example of the cousins on his mother's side, chosen to go to prep school.

It is at this point that parents can fall into the trap of listing, with "humor" and not-so-gentle sarcasm, those traits of their child that are grating and unpleasant. I don't find that to be very useful. Or we say things like, "insanity is hereditary; you get it from your children." Another trap is to take a child's accom-plishments personally and out of social context. That one goes like this: "Oh, gee, I'm so proud of your rock band. Imagine how good it feels to hear your band described as a combination of black death and the angel of death, creating a super virus." In fact that is precisely what one review of Will's band said. I was delighted!

I see no use for such self-conscious parental posturing. It only widens what is already a nearly unbearable gulf between parent

and child. I'm a dancer now and I have seen the difference between "ego-dancing" and "selfless-dancing." It is clear that there
is also ego-parenting and selfless-parenting. It's a more difficult
dance, this parenting one, loaded with fears and expectations as
it is. The line between the two types of parenting is blurred.
Selflessness morphs into martyrdom or vanity with ease.

There was one startling moment in Will's childhood that reveals
such vanity as insubstantial and delusional. He and I were playing on the family-room floor in our fine old house Sugaree. It was
a big room filled with light. There had been a blizzard the day before and snow was banked up to two feet deep on the deck. Will
was four years old. At one point during our gentle tussling about,
he stopped, dead still, and fixed me with a startled look, as if a
door had opened to the universe and he had heard a truth whispered from some far-off and trustworthy place.

He said, "Dad, I'm glad I chose you and Mom."

Amen.

We have failed our children, many of us. I did for many
years. Driven by our selfish desires for things, for comfort, for
what we considered to be safety and stability, we have hardened
our hearts. We have been angry and judgmental and afraid. We
have learned to hate other people because they are not like us.
And we have been ignorant of the truth. That truth, which we
lost sight of, is that we are all a lot more alike than we are different. In our ignorance, we began to think of ourselves as separate
individuals, with no connection to each other or to this vast and
wonderful earth. I don't think that is so. Will would not be here
if it was not for his mother and me, and we would not be here if

it were not for our parents and all the ancestors who preceded us. Pauline and I are not so important in this larger web of being.

There are other deeper connections that we often fail to see. When we are babies, the whole universe supports us. We eat food that was grown by people we have never met. And that food could not have grown if it was not for the sun and the rain and the soil that supported it. That rain, sun, and soil are all dependent on the movement of planets and galaxies and mysterious forces that none of us can really see or understand. Each little bite of baby food that we are given, on those tiny spoons, has come to us through the "interbeing" of many people and of many natural events.

As babies this is true. We are very dependent then. But do you think it is not still true? Of course not. But many of us have forgotten what we might have known as children. This morning I had hot tea and rye toast with butter and strawberry preserves for breakfast. The tea was grown in India, under the same sun that was lighting up my backyard. When I can pause to really look at the food on my plate, I am struck with the way that all things are connected. Now we have heard of such mysteries of "dark matter" and "dark energy"; the universe becomes yet more beautiful and more mysterious. At every moment of every day, whatever is happening is, truly, a mystery. There are millions of causes that make up the present moment. Without any one of them, things would be different. Our struggle at times is to see that things, right now, could not be any other way. When we can see that, we can be happy.

After my book *Cool Water* was published, Will took a great interest in the whole process of publishing and writing and even the marketing of books. He wondered why my book was called *Cool Water*. I told him what I had never told anyone to that date: the title didn't mean a damned thing; it was just the name of a song I had loved when I was a child.

On one auspicious day, in the spring of 1997, Will came into my office in our new home in the woods near Chester, New Jersey. The peach tree outside the picture window was just blossoming. Wild turkeys were feeding in the field next to the house, the dominant stag strutting and watchful. Will held a piece of stiff drawing paper. On it was a pencil drawing of a tea bowl on a narrow shelf, steam rising. Below the picture was my author name, William Alexander, and above it the title of what Will said just had to be my next book: *Silver Tea*. When I asked him what that meant he said he just liked it. Like father, like son. He didn't know what the book was about, but I promised I'd write it anyway.

In the spring of 2000, Will and I went to the island of St. John for a little vacation. My heart was heavy then. Will's mother and I had already decided to divorce but were waiting to tell Will and his three half-sibs when I was ready to move out.

We swam and ate like pigs. We rented a jeep and drove everywhere one can drive on that lush little island. We found a roadside stand that sold Ben and Jerry's ice cream and Sobe Tea.

At lunchtime on what turned out to be another pivotal and auspicious day, we were wandering to our table on the open verandah of the beachside restaurant at our lodge. I was wrapped up in some thought process or another and didn't notice at first that Will was pulling at my shirt and telling me that "that woman over there" was trying to get my attention. I saw my friends Susan and Dave (not their real names). They motioned to us to join them. It turned out that Susan had just finished reading *Cool Water* and it became the focus of the conversation. At a lull, Will jumped in and told them that my next book was going to be called *Silver Tea* and that it was his idea. They didn't have to know what the title meant, happily, but went straight to the other question: "What's it about?" Who knew?

At lunch, the conversation turned, reasonably, to alcoholism. I don't think many alcoholics have an easy time not talking about it when the opportunity comes up, or even when it doesn't. Susan, in particular, talked about the genetic component, which ran wild in her family as it did in mine. We continued in that vein for a while, overlooking the plates of good food in front of us. Finally, whether out of boredom or a desire to bring it all to close, Will said, "Okay. In other words, I'm screwed, right?"

It took the three adults several minutes to quit acting like children, so wild was our laughter.

This book, *Silver Tea,* had to be a gentle and deeply honest book about addiction. It had to be personal and it had to be honest. I wanted to pass along my father's legacy. It wasn't going to be easy. It had to be like water, not rising above, but staying in the low places. All that remained was to figure out how to structure it.

Time passed and I still hadn't written the book. Will headed off to prep school. I moved to Florida. Nothing changed and everything was different and new. It was the first separation for us and it was often difficult and more often rich with possibility for us both. The time we spent together was intense and joyous.

I still hadn't started the book.

During the holiday season of 2003, I was at odds with myself about what to give Will for Christmas. Another guitar, a Dobro maybe? Nope. What about *Silver Tea*? A few years previous I had published two daily affirmation books, one for men and one specifically for fathers.

Got it!

On Christmas Day that year one of Will's gifts was a note from me, promising that I would write him a letter every day for a year, and post it on my Web site. I did so. I missed only two days. A Zen teacher called this endeavor "wisdom that is discovered by a father as he writes to his son." I think so. I was able to look more closely at the events of our intertwined lives and write about them, after meditating. Writing *Silver Tea* became the most perfect discipline I had ever experienced. I realized, quickly enough, that this was a love letter.

The Swiss psychiatrist Carl Jung said: "Where love rules, there is no will to power; and where power predominates, there love is lacking. The one is the shadow of the other."

A day at a time, I had found a will to love and a Will to love. I invented a few characters, Sifu Pickup and JoJo Beausoleil, to say what I didn't want to say. I told stories and I told a few lies and on many occasions, I had a lot of often-wicked fun. It was an endless spiritual practice.

I have continued to write those letters, every day, right up to this moment.

Like awakening, the will to love continues to unfold. I learned that a parent whose motivation is power is a parent in whom love lies dormant. Will is not an extension of me; he must find his own way. My job, I reckon, is to serve him, not to determine what he "must do." Shunryu Suzuki, also quoted in chapter 2, said that to control your cow you must give it a large pasture. Writing these daily letters has given me the opportunity to move the fences back, to expand the boundaries of the temple. When I serve another, I am working at their level. If I "help you," I am putting myself above you and exercising power rather than love. It's tricky. It's way tricky.

Here's a view from a different corner of the pasture. It is true that if there is a large pasture, somewhere there is a corral. If a child is going to be out there roaming the pasture, that's a good thing. There are times when I have to bring my son back to the corral and hold him close, when I sense beasts out there that he can't see yet, stalking in the dark places. There are times when a child gets exhausted out there; the responsibility is too great and the outcomes too uncertain. The corral is always open.

Part of the purpose of this larger book is to grapple with the idea of atonement. I've said that atonement is at-one-ment, becoming intimate with past and present to amend those behaviors and ideas that are not beneficial to self and others. There is, as well, the atonement where we pay back money we owe, apologize to those we have harmed, or set right a bad situation we have created. The at-one-ments are also about creating harmony with God, self, and others and are useful for leading an enlightened life.

There's more.

In writing the letters to Will, I have been taken deep into my

past and have had a good look at the conditioning of my ancestors for many generations back. When I was first sobering up, I
did that, as most of us do. But there was much more that still lay
hidden, under the rocks my teacher turned over.

I have looked hard at the men in my family in particular and
have found a troubled lot. All families contain afflictions; it may
be alcoholism, cruelty, violence toward children, or the more
subtle afflictions of a lockstep conformity with the status quo or
a focus on "getting and having." What I found in my family was
alcoholism. What I found was generations of children grown to
adulthood who were afflicted with the "sins of the fathers." This
is just what is. It's not wrong or right.

So, is Will "screwed"? And what about the other children
from alcoholic families out there—screwed as well?

I don't think so. Will might be the first in my family to come
unscrewed from this devastating illness, without having to feel
its wrath.

My atonement for my past and my bloodline past could be
simply this: to stay sober and to let Will see the rewards of following his heart rather than falling into the delusional trap of
your fate. Fate is a myth, nothing more. Will has the power to
change his life at any moment, right where he is. I did it.

I was the first in my family to be liberated from alcoholism.
Since I sobered up, a few more family members have joined in.
At a deeper level, I have had the intuitive realization that when I
became free, I liberated my ancestors as well.

To the best of my ability, I have made amends for my often
gruesome behavior and have, in the words of AA cofounder Bill

Wilson, "move[d] on to a life of greater purpose." I have made peace with the past and I have done the best I can to amend my behavior and my thinking right here and now.

Is that enough?

I don't think so.

The principal affliction of my bloodline is alcoholism and its devastating effects on family, friends, and culture. Will's half-sister Kamala is a woman of great accomplishment and authentic spiritual depth. When I look at the harm that I did to this woman, when she was a child, I know that a balanced scorecard is not enough for me. I have learned this from my son and, more achingly, from his peers whose lives are still touched deeply by active addiction. I learned a different lesson from Kamala, whose generosity of spirit has allowed me back into a life, which I left for sixteen terrible years. Kam taught me that atonement is possible, even after a wrenching separation. This is true.

My son and my daughter have taught me that where I have been involved in the greatest suffering is where my work is. That realization led me to my final task, even now, on the downslope, a task begun at age sixty-two. But Will started it when he walked into my office facing that peach tree, and told me what my next book had to be. Those letters I wrote have become an unfolding book, available to anyone who wishes to see them. Those letters led me, inexorably, to my vow to put an end to the cycle of drug abuse in families.

For this work I am doing now, I am particularly grateful for the example of my new friend the mendicant Zen monk Claude AnShin Thomas and of the Buddhist monk Chuan Zhi Shakya, whom I have never met.

When I made amends and did restitution for my lying and cheating and stealing and have looked deeply at the causes and set out on my new road, all I have done is bring the scorecard to zero. The very seeds within that created such misery and havoc are still there. At the zero point I believed, often with good cause, that I had settled my debts. But the trickster, the wraith, is always there. I must go more deeply into myself and burn out those roots, through action, if I am to be loving where once I sought power, honest where once I was a thief, open where once I was closed, and nurturing where once I was exploitative. I must continue to move the walls of the temple outward and wander into that larger pasture.

The most important thing in my life is moving past zero. Happily, it is not so difficult. All that it requires is the aspiration, the practice, and the reality of the ongoing awakening. The happiness is that moving past zero is intimately connected to that aspiration, that practice, and that reality. As in the teachings of Dogen Zenji, there is not a "moment's gap" between them. The practice and the awakening "inter-are" in Thich Nhat Hanh's brilliant phrase.

It is here where sobriety, atonement, and unfolding enlightenment meet. Like Will and his mother and myself at the moment of his birth, there is just the One.

CHAPTER ELEVEN

Moving Past Zero

I have a close friend on the West Coast who has been sober for over thirty years and who has been a devoted Zen practitioner for nearly all of that time. The following is his morning schedule.

He gets up at 4:00 a.m. and is at his Zendo in town by 5:00. At 5:10, with the members of his community, he sits in meditation *(zazen)* for fifty minutes. This is followed by extremely slow walking meditation *(kinhin),* which is followed immediately by another forty minutes of *zazen.* Then, as he puts it, with "our minds quiet and calm as a forest lake" they chant the following repentance verse, which is also known as the Gatha of Atonement, three times:

> All my past and harmful karma,
> Born from beginningless greed, hate, and delusion,
> Through body, speech, and mind,
> I now fully avow.

Then, and only then, do they "take refuge" in the three jewels of Buddhist practice: the bringer of wisdom, the wisdom itself, and the community of support for embodying that wisdom.

I have chanted that Gatha, in a slightly different form, many times but when I heard of this particular way of practice, I was struck by the sense of incredible vulnerability and openness that it entails. First the group meditates in silence, gaining that sense of stillness of the waters of the forest lake. This is a state of expansive and calm awareness. In this type of meditation there is only the stillness. There are no balloons of iridescent light surrounding the meditator, no travel to distant and ephemeral lands. Such shenanigans are just projections of the ego, the small self, the troublemaker itself.

Here, there is only stillness and vulnerability. Then those shattering phrases of the Gatha: "harmful karma [actions]" and "greed, hate, and delusion." They "avow" these poisons of the mind, meaning that they own and acknowledge them entirely. There is no equivocation here. This is pure at-one-ment with the deepest reality of past sins. My friend tells me that since he began this practice (after many, many years of devoted Buddhist practice), he was challenged at a new level and was left wondering how he could, in fact, "repent."

He took this query to his teacher in *dokusan* (face-to-face teaching) and the teacher said that when an alcoholic admits to his alcoholism, he has already repented. I understand this fully. My friend has had the same experience that I have: sitting on his cushion he saw, clearly and unexpectedly, that when he got sober all of his ancestors sobered up as well. That is an immensely powerful realization.

The repentance is complete; the atonement is done; the service has just begun. Now is the time to move past zero. My friend now teaches meditation to senior citizens and has worked in prisons and halfway houses. The boundaries of his temple are clear and, having known him for nearly twenty years, I can state with certainty that the expansion of those boundaries isn't over yet. Every day, he and many like him begin anew on the path of enlightenment.

My atonement ultimately took another form. Inspired by my friend and by my days on the cushion as a formal Zen student, I now chant that same Gatha every morning. Like him, I vow each evening to "save all sentient beings" and to end desire, master the teachings, and become like the Buddha himself. Our vows are the same, but just like the recitation of verses for the Koran, the twenty-third psalm, the hidden practices of inner-alchemy Taoism, or any of the other great wisdom traditions, those vows are different, depending on who is chanting them. My friend and I cannot chant the same vows, ultimately, although they sound the same. If he and I are enjoying sharing a single cup of coffee, from a heavy white china mug, say, sitting outside on a perfect spring day, it is not the same coffee, not the same mug, not the same perfect spring day. He and I can only see what we see and taste what we taste based on our own life experience.

My fulfillment of the vow to save all sentient beings and my inner response to the Gatha of Atonement are uniquely my own. In my case, over time, I came to see that I was called to put an end to the cycle of drug abuse in families. In your situation, the call to service will be different as well. The only way to know the path of atonement, true atonement, is to just sit there. It will come to you, if it hasn't already.

Six months after Will was born, I felt the first stirring of a vow that I would not see fully for another fifteen years of practice. At that time, I undertook a study of drug abuse prevention programs and attitudes in this country. I wrote the report, finally, and dedicated it thusly: "For Willie, my son, at six months, in the hope that your world will be restored to sanity and that studies such as this will be only the artifacts of a darker time." Sadly, the times are far darker now than they were then. I once commented to my teacher that the world is a mess and she responded, "The world is always a mess." True, that is the nature of the world, but oh the darkness now.

I had a boy who was growing up in an addicted culture and I was concerned. The years moved on, he grew, things changed. Over the years, I had many ideas about how to scratch the itch. At one juncture, I was going to open a treatment center based in Buddhist principles. At another, I was going to go on the road with a bunch of fellow actors and perform fairy tales and wisdom stories anywhere we were invited. (I still like that one.) There were more, but my dreams were only dreams, and grandiose at that.

Then came *Silver Tea*. Then I met Claude AnShin Thomas.

Claude AnShin Thomas is a veteran of the Vietnam War. He was highly decorated while there and was grievously injured. The physical injuries healed, but the deeper psychic ones continued, gnawing at him until he collapsed emotionally, became addicted to alcohol and other drugs, and was, for a brief period, homeless. He was, by his own admission, still living in a state of war.

Once he stopped drinking and taking other drugs (and stayed stopped), and once he came into a more direct contact with Buddhist practice (through the Vietnamese Zen Monk Thich Nhat Hanh), healing and transformation could begin to take place. I am not going to tell Claude AnShin's entire story here. That is his right and privilege. His book, *At Hell's Gate: A Soldier's Journey from War to Peace,* does this very well. It is, in my estimation, one of the first spiritual classics of the new millennium. This book articulates what he has done with his realization, the commitment not to run from his injuries but confront them directly and with compassion. He has become a mendicant monk, traveling the world, embodying peace. Claude AnShin is committed to ending war in his lifetime with the full understanding that the first step in this process is to end the war in him. Co-arising with this practice is more and more awareness of the issues of violence in the world. It was through his greatest wounds that the peace of the Buddha was able to manifest in him. The wounds are healing, but the scars remain. His atonement, a word he uses often, is to be an instrument of peace. This is moving past zero.

It was when I first encountered Claude AnShin (through the kindness of the very man whose morning practice is outlined above) that I knew where I had to go and what I must do.

The following briefly outlines what I have sworn to do: During my lifetime I vow to put an end to the scourge of addiction in families. I know that to do so, I will have to begin with myself, seeking out the deepest roots of my addiction.

I will go anywhere I am asked to go, to talk with any one person or any group about the experience of a life of exploitation and a life of nurturance, as I have lived it thus far. I will offer only my naked experience of addiction and the severance from the earth, and of my recovery and the reconnection with the earth.

This is not new for me. I have been leading workshops for several years, at Hazelden, Esalen, and elsewhere. What is new is the focus on families. Also new is the determination to seek out new venues for this protean work. I will continue to expand the boundaries of the temple, with no certainty as to where it will end. There is no fee structure for this work; I will only accept donations, either from individuals or entities that sponsor such workshops. This is in the spirit of *dana* or generosity. If I am to serve those who ask me, I must be willing to be served by them in turn. A close friend once commented that the various ballroom gurus seemed to do two things well: create an atmosphere where people encountered their own demons without learning what to do with them, and create a dependency on the gurus themselves. I'm not so sure that's true, but I'm not going to test it. I have enough problems with grandiosity and avarice as it is.

It is just another vanity to say that as I am healed, the earth is healed, precisely as I have done in the previous chapter. "Don't tell me, show me" is the cry of Zen masters and all the great teachers. My son doesn't describe playing the guitar, he plays it, with his *shin* engaging his full body and mind. My friend Jim doesn't stand over his tiny patients in the brightly lit surgical suite and describe the healing of ear, nose, and throat problems, he just goes in there, with no-mind, and does the healing. I tell my stories, sure, those are important for this work and I am a storyteller in the first place. But I do not offer prescriptions or programs trapped forever on paper. I look at the situation that I am in and I offer my help, for whatever is asked for. I do not leave these workshops or talks with people wondering what's next. I leave them with their own ideas, brought to light by our time together.

That's my way of moving past zero. There are examples everywhere if you know how to look.

Here, for example, is the intention of my friend Dennis. Like Claude AnShin, Dennis was a crew chief on assault helicopters during the Vietnam War. He stood in the open door of those helicopters and fired at will at those on the ground. His post-traumatic stress disorder haunts him to this day, making it difficult, if not impossible, for him to leave his home on days when the weather mimics the weather of his worst days in Vietnam. Like Claude AnShin, Dennis has had serious problems with alcohol and other drugs. He has seen the suffering of his fellow veterans and has vowed to walk the length of Florida, on the small roads and through the dangerous swamps so reminiscent of Vietnam, seeking out homeless Vietnam vets and offering them the fruits of his boundless compassion, however it might manifest itself, from person to person. He will offer his wisdom and experience, face to face: the clearest expression of love.

The legacy of my addiction is reactivated every morning when I chant the Verse of Repentance. It's the only way I know to continue along this path of unfolding enlightenment. My path is my own. Claude AnShin's is his own; my friend Dennis has another; my Oregon friend, Hugh, another; my dear friend Elene another; and every Buddhist monk and every schoolteacher and every cleric and every person who works from the heart and from the gift of the deepest wounds has their own. What is yours?

On a recent trip to Atlanta, I was told a tale about a Tibetan Buddhist monk who had entered the order when he was very young. This man "has" very little. He teaches at Emory now and travels about, illuminating the teachings of the Buddha. Like Claude AnShin, he has taken a vow of poverty and is a mendicant monk. He can carry everything he has in a small duffel bag. Someone once asked him, quite seriously, why he did what he did, considering all that he had given up. He answered at once, "I do it for the joy that's in it."

Amen.

CHAPTER TWELVE

The Return

I believe that the spiritual life is not about transcending the ordinary but about entering fully into it, without discrimination or judgment. By embracing the ordinary, with the mind of love, the ordinary becomes sacred. I believe that to be so and yet I remain full of judgments and discriminatory thinking. This versus that, good versus evil, right versus wrong, dark versus light. I know that each contains the other and a large part of my spiritual practice is to realize that, to make it real, in my heart and mind.

One of my strongest judgments, fully stated earlier in this book, is that there is no such thing as significant coincidence, divinely inspired. But I am not so sure. Who am I, after all, to listen only to the teachings of other bipeds with seven holes in their faces? I have learned that I need to listen to the creatures with claws and talons and fangs and fins. I have received memorable lessons from the apparently unloving flora of the planet, especially that giant redwood in Oregon. Why would I consider these co-inhabitors of the larger self to be insignificant? Why should I consider, furthermore, that they communicate only in ways that make sense to me? What if they are, in fact, capable of conforming to the proven laws of physics and of communicating over vast distances, instantly? To accept that idea is certainly no less challenging than to accept without question that there is an unnamable and immanent power in the universe whose voice I can hear only in my own silence, often carried by just these other sentient and insentient beings. I haven't gotten to the point of talking with rocks, thank you, but who knows what's next?

I have learned from a poisonous snake and a playful dolphin and a towering redwood tree, after all. Is it possible that such communication was intentional? I don't know, but I am beginning to believe it to be so.

These beings have taught me that the spiritual future is not stuck in churches or synagogues or temples and that it is not a matter of rule and law born of isolating prejudice and fear. I believe that the future of religion, that is, the future of that which connects, is a universal spirituality, based in the earth. I won't see that in my lifetime and I doubt that my children's children will see it either. But I do believe that it is what's next. If we make it. After the past centuries' warfare, holocausts, and environmental disasters, I have to assume that a course correction is on the way, even in a culture such as ours, lost in Thanatos.

Over the period of twenty years or so of my sober life, I have had many encounters with what I can only see as the erotic life of the planet. I believe that such connection is a fair indication of the coming universal spirituality. If we make it. For addicts this erotic and ecstatic connection is especially potent as it is just the sundering of that connection that, I believe, created the plague of addictions that has swept the earth, particularly in the past hundred years. And who among us is not an addict? A Zen monk who is a great friend once said, "I am in recovery from an addiction to self."

There is one more story about this connection that I wish to tell, and it is this story that tells me that my feelings about coincidence may be just as short-sighted and distancing as my previous fierce adherence to the scientific explanation was.

In the fall of 2003, when I had first encountered T'ao Ch'ien and the poem I have quoted in these pages, I was deeply touched by the phrase "simple-hearted contentment." I wanted to have a material reminder of that phrase and I knew where to turn. Two years previous I had met, in cyberspace, a talented and soulful calligrapher named Nadja Van Ghelue. At our first meeting, she lived in Minorca and has since moved to Mallorca, Spain. She has trained with great masters of *shodo* (the way of the brush). Her devotion to this "way" is complete as she continues to embody the practice that she describes as the finger that points to the absolute.

Nadja had made one piece of calligraphy for me already and I wrote to her and asked if she could brush this simple phrase for me. Of course she could, she told me, but she would need some time to research it and to make this phrase and its expression part of her, to become at one with it. I had thought this might be a process of a few weeks, forgetting how long it had taken me to get to even the scarcest sense of the sacred through meditation and martial arts. I heard from her next in March of 2004, during the spiritual meltdown that I described in chapter 4.

Nadja had searched the literature of calligraphy to find inspiration for this piece. I later found out that she had contacted many calligraphers worldwide in her search. Here is what she told me in a gentle and loving letter: "The style I would use would be based on the work of the Chinese calligraphy-saint Wang Hsi-chih, who was a contemporary of T'ao Ch'ien. With the inspiration of Wang Hsi-chih I relink myself to the calligraphic time-spirit of T'ao Ch'ien's epoch and can achieve an evocative simple-hearted contentment." I wonder, how many of us bring such single-minded intention and power to our work? I wonder, how many of us do work that provides such spiritual insight, such unfolding enlightenment? It is folly for me to compare myself to anyone. I know nothing of their life experience. But when I encounter an artist of Nadja's power, I am humbled and inspired.

The days and weeks passed. In late May, just as I was beginning to emerge from the dark, the calligraphy arrived. She had done two pieces, a large one for me and a smaller one for Will, for the time when he would want such a reminder in his dorm room or home. They are of the same characters, of course, but are strikingly different, a testimony to the power of attention and heart she brings to all of her work in the inspiration of the present moment. Here is part of what she told me of the "birth process" of this towering work.

My aspiration was to get nearer to the spirit of the hermit. So I decided to use a twenty-year-old Chinese ink, which has a slight blue tonality. Contrary to the black Japanese sumi, which radiates outward, this blue ink goes inwards. And I thought that this matches the true sense of simple-hearted contentment . . . My idea of the calligraphy was to get an interaction of emptiness and fullness in the brush stroke, and to achieve this interaction I used a big Japanese horse hair brush. As I was rubbing the inkstick, three birds of prey were praying in the blue open sky and the youngest was making beautiful shouts of joy. I think it was a very auspicious sign of connection with T'ao Ch'ien.

Amen.

Nadja and I had talked about our matching hermit lives, in spirit at least, and of our convergence with the spirit of T'ao Ch'ien. She included another note, dedicating the calligraphy "to my hermit poet." I have reproduced her note, above, exactly as she wrote it. I have not known whether or not when she wrote "praying" she might have meant to write "playing" and I don't care. I have left it as is. The birds were praying, in my estimation.

A few more months went by and my recovery was nearly complete. On a fine summer afternoon, I was sitting on my porch, drinking ice tea and thinking about nothing at all. I had wondered, for some time, what was next, what I was going to be called to do. I was at rest but engines were churning somewhere inside of me, eager to get to work or to play or both.

All at once, three birds of prey began praying above the trees, only a few dozen yards away from where I sat, suddenly in an open connection with the larger world.

The youngest of the three was keeping his distance and was "making beautiful shouts of joy."

I knew only this: that my life was, from that point on, to be lived in simple-hearted contentment and that this was an awesome charge. I wrote to Nadja about this coincidence and she replied quickly saying that she thought that perhaps T'ao Ch'ien had "completed his journey" to my heart.

I wonder what communications went on, planetwide, encompassing heaven and earth, that led to that startling moment? What connections, deeper than thought, brought those birds of prey to my home? They had never been there before and they have yet to reappear.

Perhaps some day I will know that, but it is of little matter to me now. At last I could live immersed in the mystery and uncertainty of the ordinary and feel the reality of a life that is, in the words of the book *Alcoholics Anonymous,* "happy, joyous and free."

As the days moved on I began to sense one message from T'ao Ch'ien, while sitting out there by Hogtown Creek. It is this: I believe that it is time for a new metaphor for the life of the spirit. It was in the first Axial Age that spirit moved into heaven and it has been the aspiration for a life of the spirit, in heaven, that has informed our spiritual searches ever since. The common metaphor was of a mountain and, more specifically, of the spiritual search being a climb up a mountain, with all its difficulties and challenges to arrive at last at the summit, enlightened. And alone.

There are shelves full of books supporting this very useful metaphor, from Thomas Merton's *Seven Storey Mountain* to the parable of *Mount Analogue,* as enigmatic a book as I've encountered. We look to the mountains for strength and in many and varied religious practices may envision ourselves as mountains, solid and still. Chomolangma, in Nepal, is the tallest mountain in the world and is now littered with the detritus of climbers and, indeed, with the bodies of many a failed climber, forever frozen above the terminal moraine. Chomolangma, also known in the West as Mount Everest, is seen by Tibetans as the Mother of the Universe. Chomolangma and its sister mountains, Mount Kailas, in Tibet, and Chomolari, in Bhutan, are revered by the indigenous people, and Mount Kailas is often circumambulated by pilgrims, but rarely climbed.

I believe that now it is time to see the life of the spirit as movement down a mountain, from the isolation of heaven to a new destination: the rich and nourishing matrix of the earth, the place of origin.

A few years ago, in Atlanta once more, a therapist took me through a visualization process in which I was first asked to, ever so slowly and completely, construct in my mind a picture of my spiritual habitat at that very moment. She was very skilled and offered no suggestions at all other than to let my mind roam freely until it found that spot. It was laborious, but finally I saw myself, indeed, just below the rough peak of a snow mountain, ragged and windswept. She let me linger there awhile and then asked out of our shared silence, quickly and with great force, "Where do you see yourself next?" That one came instantly. There I was, in a lush swamp, streaked with sun through deep green foliage and black waters and humming life and there, the gods help me, only a few feet away, stood Yoda! Yoda! With that damned enigmatic smile on his puckered little face.

I told the therapist and when we both stopped either laughing or crying, whichever it was we were doing, she said, "Well, I guess you've found your Higher Power!" Yep, and I found him in the low places, in still waters. (Shortly after I moved to Florida, I found a statue of Yoda on eBay, one manufactured by Lucas Films as a promotional device, and I bought it and it stands, to this day, just inside the entrance to my home.)

The view from the top of our mountain seems infinite. The sky reaches endlessly above us and we must lower our eyes to see the nearby and lower peaks. It is achingly cold, only ice, streaked with blowing snow, and lifeless. We are far above even the sparsest of vegetation. Only the magnificent cranes of the world can fly above this place. I think of the "rocs," those mythical birds in Chuang Tzu's legend, whose backs are thousands of miles across and who fly far above the earth. Their cries echo in this cold and empty place. Climbing down from this lonely place is difficult at first. We must watch every step. Our breath, our life, is forced and difficult here. There is danger at every step, with unseen crevasses that can pitch us to a painful death, wedged in walls of tapering ice. There is no room here for mistakes; there is only the certainty of the imminence of death and the distant possibility of comfort.

This place is like no other place for beginning our pilgrimage. It offers nothing but isolation and fear. Further down, the temperature rises a few degrees and the icy path is at a lesser slope. We can still not see or rightly envision where we are going; we are driven only by a longing we cannot name. We begin to find, scattered here and there, like so many brittle sticks, the frozen bodies of those who failed at the very beginning of the journey. We wonder at this, at what could have stopped them so quickly. Was their longing for peace so great they surrendered to its seductive twin—death—and had fallen asleep here, sinking into an imagined warmth, only to find the cold, forever? Stricken with sadness, we continue down. The pitch decreases. In the distance, we see other pilgrims, inching their own paths down this formidable place. A sense of possibility dawns as we see we are not alone, although our separation from them still gapes wide.

Continuing downward, the stumbling and uncertain steps we have taken are in the past and we can walk with more confidence. The worst, we think, is behind us. We can begin to imagine this place we are going and even catch glimpses of it, beyond dense forests, which we still must pass through. We can breathe easily and treasure each breath for what it is, a gesture of life in the vast breathscape that we inhabit.

We come at last to the first signs of life, in the lichen clinging to the rocks, now exposed, free of the ever-present snow of the higher altitudes. Only a few steps further along, we encounter low shrubs and herbs, still scattered, but we can see that further down they will coalesce into fields of simple beauty. Ahead lies a boreal forest, with firs and then pines at lower altitudes yet. It is fully in view and we can rest here, for a moment, and breathe deeply. This breath, we find, is a holy thing, life itself moving in our bodies, enriching blood and flesh.

After resting, we move toward the forest lands, the earth beneath our feet becoming flatter yet and the rocks are mixed with soils and low plants. This is a place of the promise of the richness below.

Entering the forest, we can only see forest ahead, growing more dense and forbidding. This is a place of darkness, we find, and there is little comfort here beyond the rich air and soft carpet we tread. There are deep shadows and dark places and around us we can hear the scurrying of critters we have never seen. We have come from an isolated place, with blinding light, to this place of darkness and therefore have the fundamental understanding, born of experience, that there is no darkness without light.

We have formed a rudimentary theology of the earth.

In the darkness around us we sense that there are more pilgrims making this journey. We catch the scent of a rich moisture growing ahead.

Leaving the forest there is a band of sparse dry woodlands. We see lakes around us in the distance. The scent grows stronger. We have joined with other pilgrims now and are finding a certainty in the strength of this tribe. Other lone stragglers come out of the chaparral and, hesitating at first, join us.

Ahead is a plain and beyond it, we sense, the source of the scent we have just noticed. The plain is a forbidding place at first but when we look closely, remembering to breathe gently, we discover a richness of flora and fauna that is greater even than that of the forest we have left behind. We find herbs and brush in rich profusion and discover, painfully at first, that if we should fall and clutch at a plant that burns us that there is always another plant close by to ease the pain. We intuitively know this, reaching wildly in our pain for its balm.

Our theology of the earth grows deeper, twining with a mythology of journey and story.

On this plain, in the company of our fellows, we have become storytellers to share our wisdom with one another. We sit at night by fires, always near water and always in the safety of this earth, and tell our stories to one another. Each story is different, we find, although the source is the same. Moving in and out of story, we have become philosophers and tribal. We have found *telos,* and are organizing our philosophical, social and moral concerns into an ever-changing synthesis and are forming a single organism in its service.

We continue on this rich savannah, the land growing juicy and rich underfoot, until we come to the place where the waters gather, this rich swamp, the place of origin. This is the home of spirit embedded in matter, the earth mother, of which we are so inextricably a part. This is the place where heaven is below and earth is above; in the Chinese wisdom teachings of the *I Ching,* it is the place of *Tai,* or peace. This is the place of stillness *and* dancing, of dark *and* light, of love *and* death. This is the place, finally, where we can begin to live the life of no separation, the place where even the desire for simple-hearted contentment has become a vanity. Here, we are at one when we are wise enough to see it. The tribe is made of many pieces, but the tribe remains intact, always. Some die and go to that place of dark returning; some are born and enter the light without being blinded, protected as they are in the matrix of the tribe and of the earth. We listen to our dreams and heed carefully the teachings of the inhabitants of the outer rims of this swamp.

This is not yet Eden. That is elsewhere. Here there is still the suffering of old age, sickness, and death. Our *telos* evolves as our stories, lived out, become richer. It is a place of a tribal consciousness, a spiritual ecology of subtle interbeing. Our storytellers are the elders, the carriers of the wisdom stories. They are revered. It is the elders who embody the reality that wisdom, which does not transform to compassionate action, is not wisdom at all, but mere knowledge. Our other storytellers are the children, so recently arrived from places we have forgotten. It is their wisdom that reminds us of the beginningless reality of the rounds of the life of the planet, the tribe, the individual members of the tribe.

We tell our stories, we make love, we cook our meals, we dream and we tell our dreams, and we never cease in honoring our home, this earth, which waits still, always beneath our feet, and coming no more than halfway to meet us. We nurture this rich earth as it nurtures us. Gone are power, exploitation, and fear, replaced, however fitfully, with love, nurturance, and courage.

Those fearsome bridges have all been crossed, to love and to joy, and we are home.

It's amazing what happens when you climb down from the isolation of addiction to self and meaning, and let yourself come down that mountain and join up with the global tribe in your original home and join the dance of the cosmos.

CHAPTER THIRTEEN

Learning to Dance

Finally this.

My inner swamp of origin must be somewhere in the bayou country of Louisiana where the dance is zydeco. When I finally gave up on ever finding the divine in martial arts, I started dancing the zydeco form. I wasn't much at first but I kept coming back to a funky bar, downtown in my small north Florida town. Every Wednesday night, I dance. That swamp water runs in my veins, I guess, and I've found in dancing what I sought in martial arts.

There is a woman at the bar who is the best zydeco dancer I've ever seen. This woman, this Goddess of Zydeco, dances with no self, at one with her partner and with the dance itself, the form of the dance long ago internalized and forgotten.

On one auspicious evening, when the air was thick and thunderstorms threatened, this woman, Karin by name, paid a lot of attention to me. I felt singled out and it worried me. She would pull me away from my partner, for example, and make some small correction in my form. Each small correction led to a greater ease in the dance. Toward the end of the night of dancing, she asked me to dance with her, and dance we did.

She told me that there were only three things that I needed to remember. First, I was to "give weight" to my partner, meaning that my partner and I needed to lean back into each other's arms, trusting that we would not be dropped. Karin and I did that, giving each other weight, and our spins and twirls and low-down deeply funky moves were easier than I could have imagined.

Second, she told me to always face my partner directly; to never turn aside from the one I was dancing with. We did that, spinning and grinding, and Karin began to disappear, to be replaced by the dance. And, third, she told me that rather than leading with arm and hand pressure, I needed to lead from "right here," she said, pushing her hand directly into the middle of my chest, the heart *chakra,* that place in Hindu cosmology that both controls and is the source of the breath and of love. Breath and love, one thing. To love is to breathe, to breathe is to love.

When we finished our dancing together, I thanked Karin for her special attention that night, figuring that she saw that I needed all the help I could get. I was the sinner of the dance, in need of constant attention and correction. I expected judgment. What I got was mercy.

"I did it because I can tell you're going to be really good," she said.

The Goddess had spoken. All I need to do, for goodness' sake, is trust that I will be held while holding another, face my partner directly, and lead from breath and love.

Can it really be that simple?

When I set out to write this book, I didn't know where it was going to end. It seems that it has ended where it started, in love and joy, and, to my surprise, right under the wire, in that most powerful promise of the twenty-third psalm, the realization of mercy.

I think we need all the mercy we can get nowadays, don't you?

Amen.

June 16, 2005
Gainesville, Florida
Ocklawaha Bioregion

EPILOGUE

Coincidence and Atonement

On this evening, August 5, 2005, Will and I are in Santa Fe, New Mexico, at the Upaya Zen Center, for a Buddhist Ceremony of Atonement. The *roshi* at Upaya is the one person outside of my family who I have known for longer than any other. Joan Halifax is a teacher of great gifts and a friend of fierce loyalties. What a "coincidence" that in this place I would find the answer to a question I had asked everyone but myself.

This book was finished and in production. Life was good. Will and I were nearing the end of a month-long road trip, a pilgrimage, an odyssey of discovery.

Throughout the trip we had interviewed people we met. Our questions varied, but for one. We asked everyone we interviewed, "What's the most important thing?" I think this is the essential question.

I found my answer to this question—at Upaya, in the quiet of the nearby Sangre de Cristo Mountains and in the company of friends and strangers, in an atmosphere of inquiry and love and profound commitment to atonement on this day linked to the horrors of Hiroshima and Nagasaki, sixty years before.

I wrote to my editor, Becky Post, and asked that this little epilogue be added to this book, already in production. That ain't easy. Becky and I both liked the way this book already ended. But here was an answer that needed to be told. The spiritual life is personal, but it must not be secret.

The ceremony was a beautiful and simple one. I can only offer you sketches of it, so immersed was I. We chanted the Gatha of Atonement, mentioned earlier in this book. We offered incense. We, the 150 or so persons there, did 108 full bows. Will and I did them, side by side. Two statements were read. One was by a woman who is now seventy-five, who survived the attack on Nagasaki. She sat quietly as the statement echoed in the room, telling of the piles of the dead, the grating metallic boom of the explosion. The second was by a sixty-three-year-old man, just my age, who, at age three, was less than a mile from the explosion of the first atomic bomb, and who survived it. He wept as the statement was read, with its words of mankind's horror, the flesh turned liquid, the screams of the dying, the death, a few years later, of his mother, still young, from cancer.

We sat *zazen*. Then, in pairs, we approached the altar mindfully and offered incense, with the appropriate bows.

I watched my son Will, already at only fifteen a better man than I, as he reverently offered the grains of incense over the burning charcoal, and then took two steps to his right and bowed, deeply and mindfully, to this small man who was exactly my age when the world exploded into death. The bow was returned.

I saw the two of them look deeply at each other—two children for a moment, in a world of death and of atonement.

There was no great moment of epiphany. I felt mere gratitude that I had lived long enough to see such a moment. This was no awakening, no moment of shattering insight. It was only a feeling that beneath the piles of corpses, there is life, growing as from the mud of my "ancient, twisted karma." From yours, too, and from Will's.

The most important thing?

Moving past zero.

Atonement, you see, is without blame or guilt. Atonement is perpetual realignment and movement away from our beginningless greed, hate, and delusion. Atonement is the full and mindful acceptance of what is, the only soil from which compassion can arise.

I offer gratitude to Will and to Joan Halifax for this moment of seeing through, and my gratitude to you for coming along on this ride.

Happy trails.

The Twelve Steps
of Alcoholics Anonymous

1. We admitted we were powerless over alcohol—that our lives had become unmanageable.
2. Came to believe that a Power greater than ourselves could restore us to sanity.
3. Made a decision to turn our will and our lives over to the care of God *as we understood Him.*
4. Made a searching and fearless moral inventory of ourselves.
5. Admitted to God, to ourselves, and to another human being the exact nature of our wrongs.
6. Were entirely ready to have God remove all these defects of character.
7. Humbly asked Him to remove our shortcomings.
8. Made a list of all persons we had harmed, and became willing to make amends to them all.
9. Made direct amends to such people wherever possible, except when to do so would injure them or others.
10. Continued to take personal inventory and when we were wrong promptly admitted it.
11. Sought through prayer and meditation to improve our conscious contact with God *as we understood Him,* praying only

for knowledge of His will for us and the power to carry that out.

12. Having had a spiritual awakening as the result of these steps, we tried to carry this message to alcoholics, and to practice these principles in all our affairs.

How to Meditate

What I will describe here is a version of *zazen,* seated meditation from the Zen Buddhist tradition. However, there are many forms of meditation. Feel free to explore your library or to attend classes. It is useful to learn meditation from a teacher and with a group of practitioners. There is less opportunity to make mistakes this way. For example, I tried to teach myself how to play the guitar. When I finally went to a teacher, I found that I had not only learned several of the finger positions backward, I had actually perfected them. Backward. It took a lot of unlearning. In addition, it is far easier to sit for longer periods of meditation with other people than to try to do so alone and there is the benefit of a shared commitment to liberation.

The Posture

Correct posture is the foundation, literally, of meditation practice. The posture is meant to provide you with the most stable possible base. It is necessary to sit on a small pillow, called a *zafu,* or some other stable base such as a folded towel. Sit with your bottom on the very forward edge of the pillow and both knees touching the floor or ground. The cushion is used only as a wedge. Do not sit fully on it; only use the front third, so that the body is naturally inclined toward the floor and the knees can rest comfortably. The body forms a tripod. The spine is neither stiff nor slumped, simply erect. Your pelvis should be slightly tilted forward. Your upper body and shoulders are perpendicular to the floor. Be careful! There is a tendency to lean forward or back if that is what you do when you are walking and standing. Also be careful not to lean to the left or right. Your head rests straight on the top of your spine, not inclined in any direction. Your legs can be in the full lotus, the most stable posture, with the heel of each foot resting inside the thigh of the opposite leg. This is a difficult posture for most people.

Another way to place the legs is in the half-lotus, with one foot resting on the thigh of the opposite leg and the other foot on the large mat, the *zabuton,* or on the floor or rug. A far more common posture is the Burmese, where the legs are folded and the feet and knees rest fully on the ground. The right foot is drawn up close to the thigh and the left foot is in front of the right calf. In any of these postures you may place the feet in just the opposite position of what I have described; in this case the left foot close to the thigh and the right in front of the left calf. It is a good idea to switch these positions from time to time.

You may also sit on a bench or on the cushion turned sideways in what is called the *seiza* or kneeling position. Here you rest your bottom on the bench, with the legs tucked backward, kneeling, but in such a fashion that the weight of your body is borne principally by the cushion or bench.

Finally, it is entirely okay to sit on a chair. There is nothing esoteric or "better" about sitting on the floor. We sit on the floor only because it is somewhat more stable and relaxing. However, many people, because of their physical condition, temporary or chronic, need to sit in a chair. If you do, then it is useful to put a cushion on the chair, sit on the forward third of it, and rest the feet squarely on the floor. When sitting on a chair, it is tempting to lean against the chair's back and slouch. This is not such a good idea as the "lazy" posture leads to lazy meditation. Plus, it can actually become quite painful.

Remember, it is not what you do with your legs, but what you do with your mind, that matters.

It is important to remain relaxed and fully attentive. It is difficult to be attentive if the body is not relaxed. The body should be aligned and balanced, without the necessity of brute muscular strength to remain seated. If your back hurts, it is probably because you are straining to relax. At first, and often for years afterward, it is necessary to really pay attention to what your body is telling you about your posture.

Your Head and Your Hands

Sit with your mouth closed and breathe through your nose, unless some condition makes this impossible. The tongue is pressed lightly against the palate so that you won't need to swallow as often. That small detail is quite important. The eyes, usually, are half closed and lowered, focused softly on a point on the ground about three feet ahead of you. In some traditions, the Tibetan for example, the eyes are fully opened. Rarely are they fully closed. That is called "taking a nap."

Remember that all the muscles should be soft. No strain.

The hands can either be placed on the knees, palms down, as the Tibetans do, or can be joined in front of you. In the latter, the nondominant hand is placed lightly in the dominant hand and the thumbs are touching ever so slightly. If you are able to sit in the full lotus, your heels will form a natural platform for the hands. Otherwise, you might find it a bit of a strain to hold your hands this way; you might use a small pillow in your lap to rest your hands on. Just remember to relax and let the hands fall naturally into your lap. When I first began sitting, I thought, mistakenly, that the hands had to rest in a very specific spatial relationship to my navel. The pain in my shoulders finally taught me the folly of that position.

YOUR BREATH

In my lifetime I have probably only used about 50 percent of the breath I was allocated. When I am tense I don't breathe. Oddly, the only time I used to be conscious of my breathing was when I was scuba diving, because I knew how important it was not to hold my breath in that situation. When we're "uptight" our breathing is shallow, from the upper part of the chest, and it is tight. The breath is scrawny and not efficient.

When you sit in meditation, it is important to relax into the breath. Let the muscles of the abdomen relax and breathe from it, like a baby does. It is important to breathe naturally. Don't feel that the breathing is somehow "holy" or special. It is only breathing. Mere breath. Breathe gently. Don't overdo it. Just let go and let the breath flow, effortlessly. Once your posture is correct, your breathing will be perfectly natural.

When you first sit, you can say to yourself, "Breathing in, I know I am breathing in. Breathing out, I know I am breathing out." Try not to do this too often. It is just a useful way to get into a relaxed and focused breathing rhythm.

What follows is one of the favored ways of using the breath in meditation. It is not the only way, but it is what I learned and what is taught in countless classes. Simply count the breath as you sit. Count "one" on the inhalation and "two" on the exhalation, up to a count of ten, and then begin again. Here is what will happen. Soon enough, you will begin to form a story in your mind. It might be a story about how you are the only meditator in the room (if you are with a group) who is meditating the wrong way.

This story quickly escalates into a full-blown drama, with entrances and exits and a cast of thousands. Should a bell ring at a time like this, you will have a remarkable startle response. Another story, and a common one, is something like this: "I don't think I'm supposed to be thinking. Okay. So far so good, I'm not thinking. But isn't that thinking? It's like James Joyce or something. George Carlin, that's it." Loopy and totally human. So you need to make an agreement with yourself. You need to agree that whenever you find yourself thinking, you will return to the breath and start counting again at one. It is very important to just notice, very gently, that you are thinking, and return to the breath. If you make yourself "wrong" for the thinking, then you are off on the path to another drama. If you wish, you may say, "thinking" to yourself, but softly, with humor and compassion. Then breathe, starting at one. If you are really having trouble with "monkey mind," try counting backward from ten to one for a few rounds.

We are constantly talking with ourselves. It is endless. When you practice seated meditation, you become aware of this internal dialogue for the first time. You hear these voices. This is normal and healthy. It is just not very useful. At times, you may be in a crisis of some sort and one thought will continue to make its way back into the forefront of your mind. You start counting again, and here's that intrusive thought again. In a case like this, you can just let that thought run its course, without your conscious interference.

At a time of great personal trauma in my life, every time I sat I would begin to worry obsessively about where I was going to be living in the near future. I told my Zen teacher about this and she said to just allow those thoughts to run, but to promise myself that I would only indulge them for "a few minutes." I soon found that the thoughts faded quickly and were replaced by an idealized vision of the house I would like to live in. I told my teacher about this and she suggested that I vow to find that house and then to return to the present moment. I did. And I did. I lived in that very house for nearly two years before I moved to Florida.

It often takes a long while to be able to get to ten without losing track. Once you have done that, then you can practice just counting the cycle of the breath. One complete cycle of inhalation and exhalation is "one." The next cycle is "two" and so on.

After some time, you will want to simply sit, following the breath. For most meditators, the practice that we aspire to is simply breathing. It is, simply, breathing. It is very beneficial to move to this level of practice as soon as possible. Here is how to do this practice.

Take a comfortable position and gently breathe in and out to settle yourself. It is sometimes useful to make a beneficial wish for yourself and all living things. For example, you might say: "May I and all living things know freedom." After you have offered this blessing, sit quietly. Direct your attention to the thin rim of your nostrils. Notice with precision that exact spot where you are aware of the movement of your breath through your nose. It is slightly different for everyone so I will not locate it for you. It's your nose. Locate that one tiny spot and pay attention to your breath as it moves, in and out, over that spot. Pay attention only to that. You will notice that at the end of an exhalation, there is a pause before the inhalation begins. And at the end of an inhalation, there is a pause before the exhalation begins. Be mindful of those pauses. As you become more mindful, your awareness of those pauses will deepen. Don't name them. This is no longer a time to verbalize. Just notice. Breath, pause, breath, pause. Such a miracle. Observe it closely. The nose is the gate through which the breath moves. Watch the gate. As time passes, your concentration will deepen and "in" and "out" will become one thing. The "spot" where you notice the breath moving becomes the object of meditation. In this way, you are learning to pay attention, bare attention, to the present moment. Breath arises, breath falls away. In the present moment. The breath is not permanent. To hold the breath, if it could be done "successfully," would be to die. Everything changes. This is the beginning of a lifetime practice.

DAILY PRACTICE

It is important to practice daily. If at all possible, set aside the same time each day and meditate in the same place. Don't overdo it. It is not uncommon to get "high" on the idea of meditation and to want to meditate for forty-five minutes to an hour twice a day from the very beginning. That rarely lasts. It is like beginning to train for a marathon by running marathons. Take it easy. Even ten minutes a day at the beginning is plenty. After a while, you will want to increase the time. Do so. This is a wonderful and ancient practice. It will become you.

It is useful to have a special place for your meditation. Perhaps you will want to bring in a candle and some incense. A picture of a spiritual leader or of loved ones can enhance the space. Flowers and beautiful objects are also nice. But take it easy. You can end up with something so elaborate and "special" that it will become the focus of your energies and you will be stuck in the endless round of getting and having for even this simple activity. It is better to have nothing at all than to cram a small space full of "stuff."

I strongly encourage you to join a sitting group and sit with other people on a regular basis. This could be an Eleventh Step meditation group, a Buddhist group of any stripe, a centering prayer group, or any of the *vipassana, Shambhala,* or Order of Interbeing groups nationwide.

In mindfulness practice we can notice our thoughts, our feelings, our sensing, and our bodily experiences. One way to practice this at first is to make it a part of your daily meditation practice. After you have sat for a while, you can bring your consciousness to your thoughts. What are you thinking? What kinds of thoughts are most frequent? What is the progress of a thought, beginning, middle, and end? Just watch the thoughts and then let them go. How easy is it to let them go?

Next you can bring your consciousness, your impartial observer, to your senses. What do you smell now? Incense? Your socks? What are you hearing? Trucks? Birds? A buzzing in your ears from going to too many rock concerts on drugs? Touch things in your environment. What is the texture? You might bring something to eat to the cushion. Eat it slowly. Notice the sweet, the sour, and the texture. Notice closely how your tongue behaves as you eat. This is a remarkable exercise. Try it at one meal a day for a week. When you are bringing the food to your mouth, what does your tongue do? If it is liquid, what does the tongue do? If it is hot? Cold?

Now notice your feelings. Pleasant feelings are always welcome and often enhance the mindfulness process. Unpleasant feelings are unwelcome. Neutral feelings are, well, neutral. Can you notice them all, without judgment, and then let them go? It is natural to want to cling to the pleasant feelings. It is natural to want to avoid the unpleasant feelings. Notice your strategies. It is very useful to sit with an unpleasant feeling. Ride the cyclone until it blows itself out. Are you angry with someone? Sit with that feeling. Don't name it, don't judge it, just feel it in your body/mind. Let it rage itself out.

A few years ago, I became aware of a situation involved in my divorce that was extremely painful. I went into a rage out in the barn beside my house. I was losing it, so I called a friend in Oregon and asked him what to do. He told me just to sit with it and allow myself to experience the rage completely. I didn't want to do that (rage is oddly comforting at times, isn't it?) but I did it anyway. I sat, quaking with rage, and saw in my mind's eye a vision of the Buddhist saint Mahakala, the fierce manifestation of the gentle saint Avalokita, the compassionate one, who tamed him. Mahakala is one nasty-looking fellow with necklaces and a crown made of skulls. His eyes bulge and his teeth are clenched. He is the lord of the wind. There was my rage, for sure. In a nanosecond, Mahakala was transformed, in this eye of my mind, into the Pillsbury Doughboy, with that idiotic grin. I laughed aloud and tumbled off my black pillow. The rage was gone and to this day, when I feel a rage coming on, I recall that moment, giggle, and move on.

Try noticing your bodily sensations. Is your forehead hot? Cool? Is there a knot in your stomach or your shoulder? My left scapula is my greatest indicator of stress. What is yours? Can you allow it to relax? Notice your breathing. How does it change as you watch it? Do you suddenly start breathing more consciously from the diaphragm, the gut? What about temperature changes in your entire body? Label these sensations and then let them go. This is called "coming to your senses."

I have outlined a basic mindfulness practice. There are many excellent books devoted entirely to this practice. I encourage you to check them out.

Finally, please continue this practice of mindfulness meditation daily. I once heard a Zen master say that if you simply practiced meditation every day for ninety days, you would be able to maintain that practice for the rest of your life. For people who have been through addiction treatment centers, that Zen master's suggestion has a familiar resonance. The slogan in those places is "ninety meetings in ninety days," which is meant to encourage the newcomer to dedicate her energies to freedom for that period of time, with the understanding that by doing so, a bedrock of practice is established that will determine the course of her sober life. Here I encourage you to engage in this simple meditation practice, a day at a time, for ninety days. It will give you a solid understanding. And then please take it into the world. Enjoy it! If, like me, you took a lot of hallucinogenic drugs, we need to be reminded that *then* we were going on a trip; *now* we are coming home. This process of mindfulness meditation allows us to drop a lot of baggage along the way.

ABOUT THE AUTHOR

William Alexander is a writer and storyteller. He divides his time between his home in north Florida and his bit of the jungle on the Osa Peninsula of Costa Rica. He is the author of *Cool Water: Alcoholism, Mindfulness, and Ordinary Recovery,* a classic book on the art of recovery. You may contact Bill through his Web site: www.ordinary-things.com.

Hazelden Publishing and Educational Services is a division of the Hazelden Foundation, a not-for-profit organization. Since 1949, Hazelden has been a leader in promoting the dignity and treatment of people afflicted with the disease of chemical dependency.

The mission of the foundation is to improve the quality of life for individuals, families, and communities by providing a national continuum of information, education, and recovery services that are widely accessible; to advance the field through research and training; and to improve our quality and effectiveness through continuous improvement and innovation.

Stemming from that, the mission of the publishing division is to provide quality information and support to people wherever they may be in their personal journey—from education and early intervention, through treatment and recovery, to personal and spiritual growth.

Although our treatment programs do not necessarily use everything Hazelden publishes, our bibliotherapeutic materials support our mission and the Twelve Step philosophy upon which it is based. We encourage your comments and feedback.

The headquarters of the Hazelden Foundation are in Center City, Minnesota. Additional treatment facilities are located in Chicago, Illinois; New York, New York; Plymouth, Minnesota; and St. Paul, Minnesota. At these sites, we provide a continuum of care for men and women of all ages. Our Plymouth facility is designed specifically for youth and families.

For more information on Hazelden, please call **1-800-257-7800.** Or you may access our World Wide Web site on the Internet at **www.hazelden.org**.